ISBN 978-1-331-45933-0
PIBN 10193026

This book is a reproduction of an important historical work. Forgotten Books uses state-of-the-art technology to digitally reconstruct the work, preserving the original format whilst repairing imperfections present in the aged copy. In rare cases, an imperfection in the original, such as a blemish or missing page, may be replicated in our edition. We do, however, repair the vast majority of imperfections successfully; any imperfections that remain are intentionally left to preserve the state of such historical works.

1 MONTH OF
FREE
READING

at

www.ForgottenBooks.com

By purchasing this book you are eligible for one month membership to ForgottenBooks.com, giving you unlimited access to our entire collection of over 700,000 titles via our web site and mobile apps.

To claim your free month visit:

www.forgottenbooks.com/free193026

THE TERRIBLE YEAR.

FRONTISPIECE—Victor Hugo, Vol XVII, p 232.

THE POEMS

OF

VICTOR HUGO

Profusely Illustrated with Elegant
Wood Engravings

VOLUME SEVENTEEN

NEW YORK
PETER FENELON COLLIER, PUBLISHER

CONTENTS

VOLUME SEVENTEEN

LA LÉGENDE DES SIECLES

LES RAYONS ET LES OMBRES

L'ANNÉE TERRIBLE—1872

CONTENTS

LIST OF ILLUSTRATIONS

VOLUME SEVENTEEN

(6)

VICTOR HUGO'S POEMS

LA LÉGENDE DES SIECLES

SULTAN MURAD

I

A MAN was Murad, son of Bajazet,
Than all Rome's emperors more glorious yet.
Fierce lions his seraglios watched before,
Murad with murdered victims spread the floor.
White bleaching bones between the flags you
    meet,
Long streams of blood ran 'neath his sandaled
    feet;
Flooding the earth, o'er all the east they past,
And to the west their smoke and shadow cast—
Such carnage with his scimiter he wrought.
His horse a panther by the world was thought.
Smyrna and Tunis, which their Beys regret,
Like dismal corpses were on gibbets set
Sublime! The Caucasus by force and ruse,
And Libanus from Kirghis and the Druse
He took. Her chiefs, when Ephesus he sacked,
He hung; and all the priests of Patras racked.
Through Murad's victories that widely reek,
The vulture wipes his gore-bedabbled beak

Upon the jutting beams of Theseus' fane,
And wolves in Athens' street unscared remain.
The bramble clothes with green, and ivy crawls
On all those ancient desolated walls.
Tyre, Argos, Corinth, Varna cast to ground—
All mute, where echo gives the only sound.
Murad's a saint: he strangled brothers eight;
  For the last two, yet small, he chose to wait,
  And let them round the room, in ghastly fun,
  To seek their wretched mother's succor, run.
Murad, 'mid crowds he bade to feasting, sped,
  His saber in his hand; and many a head
  Flew from its trunk, as bird from off the spray.
  Ancyra, Delphi, Naxos ruined lay.
  Whole countries like ripe fruit he down will
    strike;
  People and princes he destroyed alike,
  Temples and Gods, and palaces and kings.
  Water no greater swarms of insects brings
  Than ghosts of slaughtered kings; and specters
    grim
  Around his spears unnumbered followed him.
Murad of Conquering Sultans, starry son,
  Ripped up twelve living children, one by one,
  A stolen apple in them to detect.
Murad was great: he Famagusta wrecked;
  Hilla and Megara, by Allah's aid,
  Destroyed Girgente; in their ashes laid
  Fiume and Rhodes—white slaves his harem
    needs.
  Sawed 'twixt two planks of cedar, Achmet
    bleeds—
  Such honor to his uncle's rank he gives.

Murad was wise: too long his father lives,
  So helped him off. His wives he left behind—
Daughters of Europe in whose eyes flashed
    mind,
Or Tiflis girls with bosoms white to view;
All to the waves the Sultan Murad threw,
In sacks convulsed, which th' unfathomed tide
Swept off, still struggling 'neath the ocean
    wide.
His law was to drown all; and for reply,
When by some santon he was questioned why,
"Because the women were with child," he
    cried.
Aden and Erzroom he made ditches wide;
  Modon a graveyard; and three heaps of dead
Aleppo, Brusa, and Damascus laid.
Once his own son before his arrows fell,
As target used.   He was invincible.
One Vlad refused his tribute—he they dub
(I mean the Chief of Tunis) Beelzebub—
Who the Turk's envoys took, empaled them
    straight
Each side the road, before the city gate.
On Murad came, burned harvests, barns, and
    then
The Boyard conquered; twenty thousand men
Prisoners of war he took, compelled to yield;
Next a vast wall built round the battlefield.
The twenty thousand men in embrasures,
Whence issue shrieks of torment, he immures;
For every victim's eyes he made a slit;
And when he left, upon the wall he writ,
"Stone-carver Murad to stake-planter Vlad."

Strong faith the Sultan and devotion had.
Once in Eubœa, where his lightning came,
He gave a hundred convents to the flame.
Murad, for forty years dread homicide,
Slaughtered mankind: God seemed with him
    to bide.
He was supreme unnumbered armies o'er—
Was caliph, padishah, and emperor.
"Great is Murad!" the priesthood shout the
    while.

II

Bad legislator, conqueror yet more vile,
Having around him only abject troops,
Slaves, and the crowd that in the mire stoops—
Souls tongued to lick his feet which hiding hate
Praised him for crimes, always inexpiate.
Flattered, embraced by conquered enemies,
He lived immersed in incense, pride, and joys,
With the vast weariness of worshiped wrong.

Earth was the meadow, he the mower strong.

III

One day at Bagdad as on foot he sped,
And the mean herd beheld his awful head,
What time the houses, trees, and tender sprays
Throw on the streets, oppressed by sober rays,
A fringe of shade on a large space of light,
By threshold of a cottage met his sight
A fœtid pig, whom had a butcher bled
Before he cut his throat, stretched out half
    dead.
The beast lay gasping, tortured, on the ground;

His neck gaped open with a frightful wound.
The midday sun burned up the dying boar;
And in the deep black gash, of which the gore
Close by the stall produced a smoking lake,
Each ray like red-hot steel did stab and ache.
As if at the sun's invitation, sped
Hundreds of flies that sucked the edges red;
And as around their nests doves go and come,
So flew these parasites that haunt the tomb--
Their feet in blood, their wings stretched to
　　the ray.
For death and agony and fell decay
On earth the sole mysterious evils are,
Where with the sun flies the same labor share.
The pig, who could not move, in torture lies
'Neath the fierce sun, devoured by the flies:
Quivering with pain, the hideous wound was
　　seen;
All passers-by fled from the beast unclean.
Who then of this foul woe would pity own?
The Sultan and the pig were left alone.
One, tortured, dying, cursed, infected, foul;
One, monarch, conqueror, did the world con-
　　trol,
Triumphant, high as mortal man can mount,
As if the gods had chosen to confront
The two extremities of gloom and woe.
The pig, who shuddered bones and marrow
　　through,
Groaned agonized, worn out. Murad drew near
That bleeding, shapeless thing, a sight of fear;
And as at some deep gulf you stay your foot,
He bent his head over the leprous brute,

Then with his foot in the cool shade he pushed;
And with the gesture with which kings he
    crushed,
Transcendent, Murad scared away the flies.
The dying pig opened his savage eyes,
One moment fixed ineffably his look
On him who of his anguish pity took,
Then sunk his eyes in mystery profound,
And died.

IV

    The day this on our mortal ground
Took place, what happened in the heaven was
    this:
'Twas in the solemn realm of calm and bliss,
Where light ideal 'neath th' ideal shade
Shines, and life, time, and age are past and
    fade—
Beyond what we call space, beyond the flight
Of dreams, which we below call day and night;
Place which to souls true sight of causes brings,
When viewing the now hidden side of things
You comprehend, and say, " 'Tis well; for-
    sooth,
Dark Error's other hidden side is Truth—
Chaste and white realm, where ill and dark-
    ness fade
And in whose splendor stars are drops of shade.
For what shines there is not our futile day
Of tears and laughter, birth and swift decay,
Shifting, then entering back its former night,
And like our dawn, merely a sob of light;
'Tis a divine vast day, and in the skies
By suns beheld, as in our own by eyes—

Pure day, which secrets howe'er deep can ope;
Day that would fright, but that itself is Hope,
Illuminating all the stretch of space—
Lightning by awfulness, yet dawn by grace.
All beauties there with thunders dread com-
　　bine,
Light passing thought, and shuddering glory
　　shine:
The risen from the grave fix their blest sight
On lightning splendors of the infinite.
There billowy rays like waves each other
　　chased;
'Twas on Creation's Sinai's summit placed.

The cloud was seen at moments to divide,
And dazzling brightness cast on every side;
Unfathomed depths that awful peak surround.

And the soul felt with trembling dread pro-
　　found,
Being past thought or words, in gulfs of light.
All things created shuddered—morn and night,
Angels and stars, each greatest, highest
　　thing—
Before the presence of th' invisible King,
Th' Almighty.

　　　　　He who made and blesses all,
He whom with stammering lips we Spirit call,
Goodness, Perfection, Justice, Wisdom, Force,
Beholds for aye, in their appointed course,
In timeless, passionless tranquillity,
Ages like flies in summer heat pass by.

A gulf—the earth—in darkuess, groans, and
    fear:
Far down, by thickest mists o'erspread, that
    sphere
Crept. World of gloom! where the frail hu-
    man bands
Past by and perished, as they wrung their
    hands.
India and Nile you saw, battles and frays,
Exterminations, cities in a blaze,
And ravaged fields, war-trumpets far and wide,
Europe aghast, a sword aimed at its side,
Vapors from tombs, and glare from caverns
    lone,
Eight brothers slain, and uncle, father, son;
Armies walled up, rotting, while living still;
Heads flying thick as bats that twilight fill;
Round a drawn sword fruitful of death and
    wrath,
Ripped children with their entrails gushing
    forth.
Huge stakes here smoked; there bodies close
    at hand,
In fragments sawed, mixed with the burning
    brand;
And the vast shrouder of laments and wail,
The ocean, stranded in its billows pale
Frightful black sacks, to struggle seen and
    writhe;
Crowds of wan brows, and many a fugitive;
Eyes weeping, worms, and bones of slaugh-
    tered hosts;
Whirlwinds of misty specters, and the ghosts

Shaking their shrouds. And all those bleed-
  ing dead,
From land to land in hideous chaos spread,
Empaled, to crosses nailed, to hurdles tied,
Showing their fetters, blood, wounds, tortures,
  cried,
" 'Tis Murad! Justice, Lord, we all implore!''
And at that cry, which from all quarters bore
The wind, the thunder threats terrific cast,
And flames of wrath o'er angel faces past.
The bars of hell grew red; and heaven saw
Hell's bolts, through fury, of themselves with-
  draw;
And from the fathomless abyss you see
A hand stretch forth which opened terribly.
Justice repeats the gloom, and punishment
From th' infinite was being slowly sent,
When sudden, on the cloud, from deepest night,
A beast deformed, worn out, a hideous sight,
An abject, piteous thing—a pig—was shown.
With bleeding eyes it searched for Allah's
  throne.
The cloud conveyed the pig to heaven's shine,
And placed him e'en where glows the one
  great shrine—
The Holy of Holies, where no change can be;
And the pig said, "Pardon; he succored me."
The wretched beast met the Creator's gaze.
Then, by the law which hastens or delays
His sentence who by his mysterious might
Makes dawn in darkness, and in day makes
  night,
You saw, in mists where shape distinctive fails,

Confusedly appear enormous scales.
The balance of itself comes on, and flies
Past hell wide gaping, and half open skies,
And 'neath the crowd immense of victims
    stood,
Where the vast depths of night and silence
    brood.
The Eternal eye, the only Great and True,
Beholds, as balanced there it bore in view,
In light mysterious now flashed, now furled,
In the two scales, the pig against the world.

The scale which held the pig the balance bent.

V

Murad, the mighty caliph, as he went
From out the street whose wondering crowds
    had seen
Their dreaded tyrant touch the beast unclean,
That eve a fever caught—ere morn was dead.

The Sultan's tomb of unwrought jasper made,
All gemmed; the entrance would beholders
    strike
As the inside of some vast creature like,
All covered o'er with gold and diamond.
This shrine, all other richest shrine beyond,
Bristled, as arrows in a quiver thick,
With towers above its walls of sunburned
    brick.
That tomb which Bagdad e'en at present
    shows,
Received the Sultan, and did o'er him close.

When there, and he lay stretched beneath the
    stone,
Opening his eyes he saw a light that shone,
Which seemed not of from day or torch to
    come;
A dazzling splendor filled the entire tomb.
Darkness to soft glad dawn began to change,
And his quenched eye felt a renewal strange—
A door regained for day, opening in night;
And the enormous ladder met his sight,
Which takes men's deeds to the soul-seeing
    eye.

Radiance of flames and roses did descry,
Then upon Murad's ear these words descend :—
"O Murad, son of Bajazet, attend!
You seemed forever lost, your guilty soul
One ulcer; your whole life did crime control·
You foundered among those submerged by sin.
Already Satan showed your soul within,
Condemned to join the dismal whirlwind's
    flight
Of specters, driven through the vaults of night;
You bore the wings of darkness on your back,
Hell listened for your footsteps in her track.
Drawn by your crimes, the blackness of the
    pit
Rose round you, as do mists o'er marshes flit;
You leaned above the gulf where man is lost.
But, wretch! your soul a flash of pity crossed—
Blest glow! where selfishness had ne'er a part—
Unknown e'en by yourself, possessed your
    heart.

I made you die, while right assumed her reign.
Salvation e'en the cruel can regain—
E'en bloodiest murderer, and worst of lords,
Who the least help to the least man affords.
One moment's love wins Eden repossest:
Help to a pig outweighs a world opprest.
Come, heaven opens where all glories dwell,
And thrills with joy for him who 'scapes from
    hell.
Come, you were good one day; be ever blest;
Enter, transfigured, late by crimes possest,
King! By heaven's splendors they are all
    effaced;
By spotless white see your black wings re-
    placed."

POOR FOLK

I

'Tis night: the hut, though poor, keeps out
    the wind;
The room is dark, yet something there you find
Which like a ray amid the twilight falls;
The fishing-nets are hung about the walls,
And in a nook, where pots and plates in line
Upon a cupboard shelf obscurely shine,
Stands a large bed, with curtains hung around;
Hard by a mattress spread upon the ground,
Where, like a nest of souls, five children sleep;
The hearth, where ashes still some fire keep,
On bed and ceiling cast a reddish ray;
A woman, thoughtful, pale, kneels down to pray

Their mother. She's alone; and out of doors
The ocean, white with foam, its wailing pours
To sky, night, rock, to howling winds and wild.

II

The man's at sea; a sailor from a child,
With gloomy chance doth a fierce war sustain,
For he must be afloat in squall and rain.
The children cry for food, and off he hies
At eve, when billows to the gunwale rise.
Unhelped, alone, his bark he steers and tends.
Meanwhile, the wife at home the canvas mends,
Fits on the hooks, the broken net repairs,
And for the fish-soup in the caldron cares;
Then prays to God, while the five children sleep.
He, tossed upon the ever-rolling deep,
Fares on the boundless main, and through the
        night,
Hard toil, in cold and blackness, void of light,
'Mid breakers, where the frantic billows race.
In the broad sea is the best fishing-place,
Uncertain, dark, capricious, apt to change,
Where fish with silver fins delight to range.
This spot, as their own room scarce twice as
        wide,
In a December night, 'mid fog and tide,
Upon the shifting wilderness to find,
How must he currents calculate and wind!
What plans, what skillful reckonings it takes!
The waves glide by his boat like glassy snakes,
The gulf rolls on and bursts its mighty folds,
The rigging creaks and strains, and barely
        holds.

He thinks of Jeanne while icy billows toss:
She weeps, and calls on him. So speed and
    cross
Each night their thoughts, those soul-birds,
    through the skies.

III

She prays. The gull, with its harsh, mocking
    cries,
Scares her; and 'mid the rocks, shattered by
    storms,
The ocean fills her with dismay. Strange
    forms
Pass thro' her mind—the sailors on the sea
Who swept across the furious billows be.
And in its case, like blood in th' artery,
The cold clock ticks, casting in mystery
Drop after drop, time, winter, summer's heat;
And in the boundless world each several beat
Opens to souls, that hawks or doves become,
On either side the cradle and the tomb.

She thinks and dreams. "What poverty we
    know!
Barefoot the children e'en in winter go!
Black bread alone and never white we taste!
Oh, God!" The wind roars like a furnace blast.
The coast sounds like an anvil, and you see
In the black storm the constellations flee
Like clouds of spars that from the hearth arise.
It is the hour: midnight (gay dancer) plies
Folly's wild game, with mask and glances glad ·
It is the hour: midnight (dark brigand) clad

In shade and rain, and in the stormy north,
Takes the poor shivering sailor, and hurls forth
And breaks on monstrous rocks that ocean
       crown.
Horror! the man whose voice the waters drown
Feels rent and wrecked his vessel as it sinks—
Feels 'neath him gape th' abyss and night, and
       thinks
On the old iron ring of the safe quay.

These gloomy visions wring her heart, and she
Trembles, dismayed, and weeps.

IV

                      Oh, wretched wives
Of sailors!   Dreadful 'tis to say, "My lives—
Father, sons, brothers, lover; all most dear;
My heart, blood, flesh—are in that chaos there."
Waves like wild beasts devour their human
       prey.
Oh, God! that waves with such dear heads
       should play!
With husband, master, and the shipboy child;
That the wan wind, blowing its clarions wild,
Unknits above them his long, haggard hair;
And that, perhaps e'en now, such woes they
       bear,
And that one ne'er is sure how they may be,
And that for guard against the boundless sea,
Against the gulf of night, where shines no star,
A plank, a sail, their sole protections are.
Dark Care!   They run across the shingly track;
The tide mounts, and they cry, "Give me them
       back!"

Vain words, alas! What answer can be brought
From the storm-tumbled sea to anxious thought.

Jeanne's heart is torn: her husband, helped by
    none
In that fierce night, 'neath that black shroud
    alone!
Too young the boys to help. "Would strong
    they were,"
The mother cries, "their father's toil to share;"
One day, when with their father, you will 'plain,
Weeping fast tears, "Would they were young
    again!"

V

Lantern and cloak she takes: 'tis time to learn
If the sea calms, if yet he may return,
If breaks the dawn, and if the signal shows.
She starts; not yet the breeze of morning blows;
Naught can be seen, no single line of white,
In all the gathered blackness of the night.
It rains—nothing more black than morning
    rain;
'Tis as though day with trembling doubt was
    ta'en,
And dawn, like infants, weeps and wails at
    birth.
No light from any window shines, or hearth.

Struck all at once her eyes that seek the way,
A sight that presaged undefined dismay—
A gloomy hovel, ruined all, and waste;
No light, no fire; the door sways in the blast;

The roof hung tottering on the mouldy walls,
And rent the hideous thatch by northern squalls;
The straw foul, yellow, as when waters rot.
"Hold! this poor widow I had clean forgot!
Ill and alone," she cries, "my husband late
Found her. I needs must go and see her state."
She raps and listens, but none answer there,
And Jeannette shivers in the cold sea air.
"Sick, and her hungry children! What distress!
She has but two, but she is husbandless."
She raps again. "Ho, neighbor! answer me."
The house is silent still. "Ah, God," says she,
"How sound she sleeps! In vain I knock and
        cry."
But then the door, by some deep mystery,
As though inanimate things could pity feel,
Opened itself, its secret to reveal.

VI

She entered; then her lamp its light shed o'er
The dark, dumb house beside the sounding
        shore.
Rain-torrents through the ceiling forced their
        way

At the room's end a dreadful object lay—
A woman, ghastly, still, stretched out, who had
Bare feet, glazed, sightless eyes, and scarce was
        clad ·
A corpse, once a strong, happy mother; now
Disheveled specter of dead want and woe—
All the poor leave, after their long hard fight.
Half hid upon the straw, and half in sight,

Her livid arm, her hand, already green,
Hung down, and horror sped those lips between
Whence had the fleeting soul that bitter cry
Of death thrown forth, heard by eternity.

Close to the bed their mother lay upon,
Two babes, a little daughter and a son,
In the same cot slumbered with peaceful smile.
The mother, feeling death's approach the while,
Her shawl, her gown, upon the children flings,
That, in the shadow which death's presence
　　brings,
Decay of heat she might from them withhold,
And they be warm, while she herself grew cold.

VII

How in their cradle sleep they both; and how
Their breathing peaceful is, and calm their
　　brow.
Seems it as naught those orphans' sleep could
　　fray—
Not e'en the trumpet of the judgment day;
For, blameless, they dare stand the Judge
　　before.
The rain abroad does like a deluge pour.
From the rent ceiling, which admits the squall,
At times a drop does on that dead brow fall,
And gliding to the cheek, becomes a tear.
The surge like an alarum clock you hear.
Listens the dead, as if of sense bereft;
For bodies, when the radiant soul has left,
Seem the departed one to seek and reach.
You think to hear the interchange of speech

'Twixt the pale mouth, and eyes that sightless
  stare:
"Where is my breath," "And thou, thy glances
  where?"

Live, love, and pick the primroses.   Alas!
Dance, laugh, inflame your heart, and drain
  your glass.
As every brook to the dark ocean flows,
One end to feast and cradle fate bestows;
For mothers worshiping their children's bloom,
To kisses which the raptured heart consume,
To songs, to smiles, to love so fair and brave—
The melancholy chilling of the grave.

VIII

What is Jeanne doing in that house of death?
What in her cloak's wide folds hides she be-
  neath?
What, as she goes away, does Jeannette take?
Why beats her heart, and steps unsteady quake?
Why hurry thus, and running like the wind,
Seeks her own cot, and dares not look behind?
What with so scared a look does she conceal
In darkness on her bed?   What does she steal?

IX

When reached her house, the cliffs more white
  appear,
And close beside her bed she took a chair.
Pale she sat down, self-blamed you would have
  said,
To see her in the pillow hide her head.

At times her lips uttered some broken speech:
Afar the fierce sea roars upon the beach.

"My poor, good man! Oh, God! what will he
    say?
So full of cares! What have I done to-day?
Five children on his hands—and labors so!
Had he not toil enough, that I must go
And add all this?—'Tis he.—My fault I own;
And if he beat me, it were rightly done.
'Tis he! No! Well! Yet seemed to move the
    door
As though he came. See! what ne'er was
    before—
I fear to see my good man come again."
Thus did she saddened· and in thought remain,
Plunging more deep in grief, and anguish tost,
In endless cares as in abysses lost.
She now not even hears the noise without,
Of cormorants, that like black criers shout
And fury of the winds and waves and tide.

With sudden clasp the door flies open wide,
And rays of light within the cabin lets;
The fisherman, hauling in his dripping nets,
Appeared, right glad, and said, "Your sailor's
    here!"

X

"'Tis thou," cried Jeanne. And to her breast
    as near
Her husband clasped as lovers wont to strain,
And warmly kissed, all soaked with seas and
    rain,

The while he said, "Yes, wife, I'm here!" and
    showed
In his frank brow, on which the embers glowed,
How pleased he was that safe with Jeanne he
    stood.
"I'm robbed," he cried; "the sea's a brigand
    wood."
"What weather was it?"   "Bad!"   "What
    fishing?"   "Bad!
But now I kiss you, and that makes me glad.
I've nothing caught at all, my net is torn;
The devil surely in the wind was borne.
What night! In such a storm I could but think,
As snapped my cable, that the boat would sink.
And thou, what wast thou doing all the while?"
Jeanne shuddered, at a loss, unused to guile.
"I," said she; "just as usual—nothing more·
I sewed, and heard the sea like thunder roar.
I feared—the winter's cold—'tis all the same."
She trembled like to one who feels to blame;
Then added, "By the bye, our neighbor's dead.
She died—no matter—yesterday, 'tis said,
At eve, after you started for the night.
She leaves behind two children—babies quite.
One is called William, and one Madeleine;
He cannot walk, she scarcely prattles plain.
The poor, good soul great want had struggled
    through."

The man looked grave, and in the corner threw
His navy cap, all drenched; and, as he sate,
"The devil!" twice exclaimed, and scratched
    his pate.

"We had five children; this will seven make.
Already in bad times we'd naught to take
For supper, now and then: what to do now?
Worse luck! 'tis not my fault.   And, anyhow,
'Tis the good God's concern.   These be strange
    haps.
Why did He take the mother from these scraps
No bigger than my fist?   Such haps be rude,
And need book-learning to be understood.
So small, you cannot say, 'To work betake.'
Wife, go and fetch them; if they're now
    awake,
Alone and with the dead, how great their
    fear!
Their mother rapping at the door we hear;
Let's open to her babes.   We'll mix them all;
Upon our knees at even shall they crawl,
Brother and sister to our other five.
And when He sees we must for all contrive—
For the small girl and this small boy as well—
Kind God with larger draughts my nets will
    swell.
For me, I'll doubly work, and water drink.
'Tis said: go fetch them; but you're loth, I
    think.
In general you run more quickly far."

She drew the curtain: "Husband, here they
    are!"

THE FALLS

NIAGARA—Rhine—dash down with foaming
  wave;
The monstrous gulf would fain become their
  grave.
It hates the giant river, and declares,
"I'll swallow it." The stream (as, unawares,
A lion in a hydra's den may roam)
Struggles with all its sound and storm and foam.
What then? Vast Nature's self untrusty is!
It rears, it shuns the deep dark precipice;
It foams and boils, as marble white and black;
Cleaves to the rocks, and by the trees holds
  back;
Leans, and as if by some fell fiend controlled,
Rolls over, as th' undying Ixion rolled.
Twisted, torn, conquered, God permitting it,
The shattered stream does to its pangs submit.
The gulf would kill it, but its force and hate
May chaos form, but cannot uncreate.
The frightful pit of hell opes its dark jaws,
And raves. What toil, darkness and death to
  cause!
It is destruction, envy, rage, and night;
These are the works, the produce of its might.
As smoke upon Vesuvius' summit rests,
A gloomy cloud that caldron vast invests,
And hides the torments of the mighty stream.
This, the wealth-giver, wherefore hateful deem?
What has it done to forest, mountain, field,

That to the abyss they all its life would yield?
Its splendor, beauty, goodness, strength, all be
Destroyed?   What infamy, what treachery'
Like bladder filled with wind, the waters swell;
Horror disperses its despairing knell;
Engulfment, darkness, shipwreck, all destroys;
You'd say a frightful laugh was in the noise.
Nothing is spared—naught floats and naught
    survives.
Crushed by that dreadful wheel, the river strives;
Tortured it falls, and to the distant sky
Casts a long fainting, agonizing cry,
When lo! above that chaos of despair,
Composed of all the gulf within it bears,
Torrential, hideous, hostile—there is seen
The rainbow, splendid with celestial sheen.
Vile plot! base rock! would the next stream
    entomb!
Glory, thou springest from this frightful gloom.

AFTER THE MASSACRE

[From Count Félibien in the "Legend of the Centuries"]

BECAUSE the risen town to reason must be
    brought,
Because in civil war but massacre is taught,
And misdeeds 'venged by deeds more cruel,
    doubly red,
Fierce Cosmo doth the blood of countless wretches
    shed

Pell-mell, both young and old, at one fell, fright-
ful blow,
In fair Sienna, all her glory laid so low.
The city walls are riddled through with cannon-
shot;
The massacre is finished, but the mantle hot
Of hell is o'er the town, of Lombard hosts the
prey.
Around the cannons' lips the curling smoke doth
play;
The horror of the charge and of the combat wild
Is visible in all—the brooks with blood defiled,
And even in the dead men's wild and staring
eyes,
Upon their opened lips still seem their savage
cries;
The lightning in their eyes still flashes fiery red,
So live and furious seem the cold and slaughtered
dead.

THEOCRITUS

O LOVELY one, fear Love, the smallest god,
But mightiest; dire at heart, yet radiant-souled;
Fatal his thought, his utterance honey-sweet!
At whiles one finds him cradled 'mong deep
moss,
Fearful and smiling, with bright flowers at play.
No word he saith believes he; wild sweet cries
And tears are mingled with his tragic joy.
Maia the meadow makes, the georgic he.
Love always weeping, triumphs everywhere;

Woman is trustful of the boy-god's kiss—
It pricks not, smooth as maiden's are his lips.
"Thou'lt make thy flounces damp in meadow-
    grass.
Lyde, where venturest thou at early dawn?"
Lyde replies: "To direful fate I yield:
I love, and go Damoetas to waylay;
Till falls dusk even fondly still I stay—
Till in the birch and elm 'tis almost night,
And from the fountain leaps the green-eyed
    nymph."
"Ah, fly Damoetas!"   "Trembling, I adore him.
I cannot cull him all the flowers at once,
For one in summer blooms, in autumn one—
But, oh! I love him."   "Lyde, fear Astarte.
Thy heart, a prey to somber dreams, conceal."
Yet to her mother must the fond girl tell
Her loves at early dawn, when fades the moon,
And, laughing, she awakes in her white bed.

LONGUS

CHLOE, bare-bosomed, dazzles the dim woods;
She archly smiles, bright innocence being her
    garb.
Naked she is, and loves it; lovely, nor knows.
To all dreams most adored she is most like;
The snowy lily sees her and is not vexed;
Night thinks she's Venus, Psyche, the rapt dawn.
A tender and fearful mystery is Spring!
Afloat in the air some sweet unwitting fault

One feels, which, to soft sounds of wind and
  stream,
In the soul alights, as it thrilled woods the bird.
Io Hymen! Springtide comes, by sweet surprise
Takes Nature; the divine adventure bears
Of love to the woods, to flowers, to hearts—to
  all!
The nymph web-fingered from the fountain
  springs,
In the tree the dryad, and the faun in man;
The wingèd kiss at every mouth seeks alms.

JEAN CHOUAN

THE Whites fled, and the Blues fired down the
  glade.
A hill the plain commanded and surveyed,
And round this hill, of trees and verdure bare,
Wild forests closed th' horizon everywhere.
Safe hold and rampart were behind the mount:
There the Whites halt, and their small numbers
  count.
Jean Chouan rose, his long hair floating free:
"None can be dead, since here our chief we see,"
They cried. Jean Chouan listened to the shot:
"Are any missing? No! Then tarry not,
But fly!" Around him women, children stood,
In terror. "Sons, re-entering quick the wood,
Disperse yourselves!" As swallows scattering
  fly
On rapid wings when storms invade the sky,

They fled to thickets drowned in mist and shade,
And ran—e'en brave men run when they're
    afraid.
Dread the disorder, when in trembling flight
Old men and infants at the breast unite,
Fearing or to be killed, or captive ta'en.
Jean Chouan, last, did with slow steps remain,
And often turned him back, and made a prayer.

Sudden, a cry within the glade you hear!
A woman 'mid a storm of bullets stood.
Already the whole band was in the wood;
Jean Chouan only stays.   He turns, and sees
A woman burdened.   Pale and weak, she flies;
Her naked feet, torn by the brambles, bleed;
She's all alone, and cries, "To help me, speed!"
Jean Chouan mutters, " 'Tis Jeanne Madeleine."
In line of shot, in middle of the plain,
On her the bullets with fierce fury pour.
Ah! God Himself must bend the victim o'er,
And take her hand, and shelter 'neath His wing.
Death does such numerous darts around her fling,
She must be lost.   "There, help!" she loudly
    cries;
But fugitives are deaf, and fear denies.
The balls upon the helpless peasant rain.
Then on the hill which dominates the plain,
Jean Chouan bounded, manly, calm, and proud,
Dauntless.   "I am Jean Chouan!" called he
    loud.
The Blues cried, " 'Tis the chief!" and that
    brave form,
Engrossing all the thunder and the storm,

Made Death his target change. "Now take to
    flight!"
He shouts; "save yourself, sister!" Mad with
    fright,
Jeanne sped into the wood, her life to save.
Like pine on snow, or mast upon the wave,
Jean Chouan, whom death seemed to fascinate,
Drew up. The Blues see only him. "I wait
What time your safety needs. Go, daughter,
    go!
Joy 'mong your kindred you again shall know,
Again sweet blossoms in your bodice place."
And he alone it was who then did face
The storm of shot which fell on his great
    height,
Which seemed as if e'en then would win the
    fight.
The balls fell thick as hail. With scornful eye
He smiled and raised his sword, when suddenly
As a bear struck in cavern deep and wide,
He felt a ball pierce thro' and thro' his side.
He stood, and said, " 'Tis well. Hail, Mary,
    maid!"
Then staggering toward the wood, he turned his
    head ·
"Friends! friends! has Jeanne your shelter
    reached?" he cried.
"She's safe!" the voices from the wood replied.
Jean Chouan murmured, "Good!" and dead he
    fell.
Peasants, O peasants! True, ye chose not well,
But still your memory has not lessened France.
Great were ye in your fierce, dark ignorance—

Ye, whom your kings, wolves, priests, and sav-
    age wood
Made bandits of, were valiant knights and good.
Through all your frightful yoke and errors foul
You had mysterious flashes of the soul;
Bright rays at times from out your blindness
    flew.
Hail! I, the banished, am not hard on you:
Exile!—I know the cottage roof to spare.
We are proscribed, and you but phantoms are!
Brothers, we all have battled, but we sought
The future; you, benighted lions! fought
To keep the past.   We strove to climb the height;
You strove no less to sink in gulfs of night.
All warred, and martyrs were, by different
    course,
Without ambition and without remorse—
We to shut hell, you to keep wide the tomb.
Yet on your brows from high does radiance
    come;
Fraternal love and pity can unite
The sons of day with children of the night.
And Hero of the Darkness! in this lay
For you I mourn—I, Soldier of the Day.

THE CEMETERY OF EYLAU

THIS to my elder brothers, schoolboys gay,
Was told by Uncle Louis on a day;
He bid me play, with tender voice and bland,
Thinking me still too young to understand.

Howe'er I listened, and his tale was this:
"A battle? Bah!—and know you what it is?
A deal of smoke. You rise at dawn, and late
You go to bed. Here's one that I'll relate:
The battle is called Eylau. As I wot,
I then was captain, and the Cross had got;
Yes, I was captain—after all, in war
Man but a shadow is, and does not score;
But ne'er mind me. Eylau, you understand,
Is part of Prussia—water, wood, and land,
Ice, winter everywhere, and rain, and snow.

"Well, we were camped a ruined wall below,
And round the ancient belfry tombs appear.
Benigssens' tactics were, first to come near,
Then fly. The Emperor such arts disdains,
And the snow whitened over all the plains.
Spyglass in hand, Napoleon passed our way;
The guard declared, 'To-morrow is the day.'
Old men and women fled in troops confused
With children. I looked on the graves and
        mused.
The night-fires lit, the colonel bending o'er,
Cried, 'Hugo!' 'Here!' 'How many men?' 'Six
        score.'
'Well, your entire company take round,
And there get killed.' 'Where?' 'In the burial-
        ground.'
I answered, 'Apter place you could not find.'
I had my flask; we drank; an icy wind
Blew. He said, 'Captain, death is close at
        hand.
Life's pleasant—'tis a thing you understand;

But none dies better than your jolly blade:
I give my heart, but sell my skin,' he said.
'Let's woman toast!—your post's the worst of
     all.'
(Our colonel oft a merry jest let fall.)
He adds, 'The foe from ditch and wall keep
     back;
Stay, there, 'tis rather open to attack.
This graveyard of the battle is the key;
Keep it.' 'We will.' 'Some straw will handy
     be.'
'We've none.' 'Sleep on the ground.   Now
     tell me this:
Your drummer, is he brave?' 'As Barra is!'
'Good!   Let him blindly, madly sound the
     charge:
Noise must be great when numbers are not
     large.
D'ye hear, you little scamp, what you are bid?'
'Yes, Captain,' said the grinning child, half hid
In snow and rime.   The colonel then went on:
'The battle will be fought with guns alone;
I myself like cold steel, and hate the way
In which the dastard shells are made to slay.
Valiant the sword—the shell's a traitor.   Well,
The Emperor sees to that.   Naught more to tell,
And so, good-by.   The post you will not leave,
Nor budge a foot, till six to-morrow eve.'
The colonel left.   I cried, 'Right turn!' and
     thence
We soon all entered in that narrow fence;
Grass walled around, a church amid the sod;
In gloom, and o'er the graves, the Blessed God.

"A somber yard, with many a snowy plate,
Looked somewhat like the sea.   We crenolate
The wall.   I order all things, and decide
The ambulance shall 'neath the cross abide.
'We'll sup, then rest,' I said.   Snow lay about;
Our clothes mere rags.   'Tis very fine, no doubt,
But still unpleasant when the weather's bad.
I made my pillow of a grave, and had
My feet benumbed—my boots had lost their
      sole;
And captain soon and soldier, cheek by jowl,
No longer stirred, each sleeping o'er a corse.
So soldiers sleep; they neither know remorse,
Pity, nor fear—not being in command;
And frozen by the snow, or burned by sand,
They sleep.   Besides, fighting keen joy supplies.
I said, 'Good-night,' and then I shut my eyes.
War has no time for pantomimes inept.
It snowed; the sky was sullen, and we slept.
Some tools we found, and made a mighty flame;
My drummer poked it up, and to me came,
To cast the reckoning as best he can.
Sons, a great soldier was the little man!
The crucifix looked like a gibbet vast;
The snow still fell; the fire out at last.
For how long time it was we slumbered so,
I say, the devil take me if I know!
Soundly we slept.   In sleep is death rehears'd:
'Tis good in war.   I was right cold at first,
Then dreamt, and fancied many a skeleton
And specter that great epaulets had on.
Slowly, though I upon my pillow lay,
I had a feeling as of coming day;

My lids, though closed, a sense of radiance found.
Sudden, through sleep, a deep and sullen sound
Roused me—'twas like a cannon's distant roar.
I woke, and something white was gathered o'er
My eyes. The snow, with soft and gentle fall,
During the silent night had wrapped us all
In shrouds. I start, and shake the snow away.
A bullet coming, whence I cannot say,
Awoke me quite. I bid it pass at large,
And cried, 'Drummer, get up, and sound the
    charge!'

"Then six score heads (as isles from ocean) all
Rose from the snow; the sergeant sounds the
    call.
The dawn then rose, red and with joyance glad,
As 'twere a bloody mouth with smiling clad.
My thoughts ran to my mother, and the wind
Seemed whispering to me, 'Oft in war we find
That with the rise of day death too doth rise.'
I mused; at first around all quiet lies,
Those cannon-shots only as signals were:
Before the ball, at times, some bars we hear,
Some prelude dancing with unmeaning strains.
The night had clogged the blood within our
    veins,
But coming battle made it hotly course.
The army 'gainst us came in all its force.
We held the key. A handful were my men,
On whom the shells, like woodman's ax, were
    then
About to rage. I wished myself elsewhere.
My men to skirmish, by the wall with care

I placed, who confidence and solace found
In hoped promotion, bought by grievous wound:
In war you confront death to clutch at fame.
My young lieutenant, from St. Cyr, who came,
Said to me, 'Morn, how sweet a thing I think!
How charming the sun's rays! The snow is
pink;
Captain, all laughs, and shines. How fresh the
air;
How white the fields; how peaceful, pure, and
fair!'
I answered, 'Soon 'twill all to horror change.'
My thoughts were of the Rhine, the Alpine
range,
The Adige, and our dreadful wars of yore.

"The battle burst: six hundred throats and
more,
Enormous, belching forth the fire that fills
Their mouths, together clamored from the hills;
All the whole plain one smoking gulf was seen.
My drummer beat the charge with fury keen.
With cannons mixed the trumpets proudly
sound,
And the shells rained upon our burial ground
As if they wished to kill the very grave;
The rooks desert the tower their lives to save.
I recollect a shell burst in the earth,
And the corpse, startled, rose from out his berth,
As if man's racket woke him in the tomb.
Then the fog hid the sunshine. Ball and bomb
Produced a noise dread, inconceivable.
Berthier, Prince of the Empire, Vice-Constable,

Charged on our right a Hanoverian corps
With thirty squadrons. These you saw no
     more,
Save thickest, darkest mist, starred o'er by shell,
So wholly had the strife and battle fell
Within that tragic mist been lost to view.
A cloud fallen on the earth spread round and
     grew
From smoke which myriad cannons vomited.
Children, 'twas under this the armies bled.
Soft as the down floated the snow that night.
Good faith! we killed each other as we might:
We did our best.   The dark and ruins through,
I saw my men like shadows come and go—
Ghosts, like espaliers, which on walls you range.
The field brought to me musings deep and
     strange—
Phantoms above, and the still dead below.
Some blazing cottages at distance glow
The fog, through which was heard the mountain
     horn,
E'en thicker than before was toward us borne.
We now saw nothing but our burial ground;
We had the wall at midday for our bound.
As by a great black hand, so by the night
We were inclosed, and all things fade from
     sight.
Our church some seagirt rock appeared to be.
The bullets through the fog too closely see·
They keep us company, crushed the church roof
And shattered the stone cross, and gave us proof
That we were not alone on that dread plain.
We hungered, but no soup at hand—'tis vain

To look for food in such a place.   And worse,
The hail of balls fell with redoubled force.
Bullets are awkward.   Down they rain a-pelt;
Only what falls, and is unpleasant felt,
Are grains of flame, not sprinklings of a shower.
We were like men whose eyes are bandaged
       o'er.
All fell to pieces 'neath the shells—the trees,
The church, the tower; and I found decrease
The shadows which I saw around the place.
From time to time one fell.   'Death kills apace,'
A sergeant says, like wolf ta'en in a net;
And as his sight the tombs snow-covered met,
'Why place us where already is complete
The tale of guests?'—Man's lot is like to wheat,
Thus to be mowed, and not the scythe to see.
Some shadows yet in the gloom living be;
The scamp, my drummer, still his might em-
       ployed.
We fired above the wall, now nigh destroyed.
Children, you have a garden: shot and ball
Rained on us, guardians of that fatal wall,
As you drench flowers with your water pot,
'Till six o'clock you must not leave the spot.'
This order all my thoughts were fixed upon.—
The lightnings flash 'mid feathers of the swan;
And 'mid the dark, the bullets' flaming track
Were all my eyes could see.   'Let us attack!'
The sergeant cried.   'Whom?—for I no one
       see.'
'I hear their voice, their trumpet bray,' said he,
'Let us rush forth!   Shot, shell, upon us rain;
Death spits upon us here '   'Let us remain.'

I add, 'The battle's brunt by us is borne.
We hold the key.' 'My patience well-nigh
        worn,'
The sergeant said.—Black were the fields, the
        sky,
But though full night, the evening was not
        nigh.
'Till six o'clock,' low to myself I said.
'By Jove! few better chances can be had
To advance,' said my lieutenant; when a ball
Carried him off.   I felt no hope at all
Of winning.   Victory is an arrant jade.
A pallid glare, which through the fog was
        made,
Vaguely lit up the graveyard; but afar
Was naught distinct, save that we needed air
To concentrate upon our heads the bombs.
The Emperor placed us there among the tombs,
Alone, riddled with shot, which we returned;
But what he did with us we ne'er discerned.
We were the target midmost in that fight;
And to hold good, and battle on till night,
Till six o'clock to live the hours through,
Meanwhile to kill, was what we had to do.
Fierce, powder-blackened, shot we as we might,
And took but time our cartridges to bite;
Without a word our soldiers fought and died.
'Sergeant, d'ye see the foe retreat?' I cried.
'No.' 'What, then?' 'Naught.' 'Nor I ' 'A
        deluge?' 'Yes,
Of fire.' 'See you our men?' 'No, but I guess,
From how the volleys sound, we're forty good.'
Cried a brave grumbler, who beside me stood

(He'd won his stripes), 'At most you'll thirty
    find.'
And all was snow and night; the piercing wind
Blew; and while shivering, we the rain-drops
    track,
A gulf of white spots 'gainst abyss of black.
Howe'er, the battle seemed becoming worse;
A kingdom perished 'neath an empire's force.
Behind the veil you guessed some dread event,
As lions upon mutual slaughter bent.
'Twas like the ancient giants' fabled war;
You heard discharges pealing near and far,
The crash of ruins—the outskirts of the town
Of Eylau set on fire and burning down.
The drums their dreadful music now surpass,
Six hundred cannon make the unceasing bass.

"We killed each other; nothing yet was known
By France, that hour her greatest stake was
    thrown.
Was the good God on high against or for?
How dark! I pulled my watch out o'er and o'er.
At times the silent field gave forth a cry—
Some fallen body writhed in agony;
Fast, one by one shot down, we met our doom;
Death-rattles filled the vast sepulchral gloom.
Kings have their soldiers as you have your toys.
I raised my sword, and shouting 'Courage, boys!'
I waved it o'er my head. Strife now I wage,
Intoxicated, deaf, with so much rage;
Blow following blow by shot and shell were
    dealt.
Sudden, my arm—my right arm—hung. I felt

My sword drop to my feet upon the sward:
My arm was broken. I picked up my sword
With the other hand, and, 'Friends,' I gayly
    cried,
'To get this broken too is not denied.'
Then I began to laugh—a useful whim;
For soldiers are not pleased to lose a limb,
And when their chief is wounded, rather
    glad.
How fled the time? One only hand I had—
That my sword needed, whatsoe'er betide;
The other, drenched in blood, hung by my
    side.
I could no longer get my watch. When, lo!
My drummer stopped. 'Knave, are you fright-
    ened?' 'No;
I'm hungry,' said the child. Just then the
    plain
Seemed rocked and shaken, and was filled
    amain
With such a cry as up to heaven rose.
I felt myself grow weak—the whole man goes
From out a wound. A broken arm, it drains.
To talk with some one when you're faint, sus-
    tains.
My sergeant spoke to me. At hazard, 'Yea,'
I cried; I did not want to faint away.

"Sudden the noise left off; the night less black.
'Victory!' they shout. I shouted 'Victory!'
    back;
And then some lights approaching us, I see.
Bleeding, upon one hand and either knee

I crawled, and cried, 'How do we stand?' and
    then
I added, 'All rise up, and count, my men.
'Here!' said the sergeant. 'Here!' my scamp
    replied.
The colonel, sword in hand, stood by my side.
'Tell me by whom the victory was gained.'
'By you,' he said. The snow with blood was
    stained.
'Hugo, that's you; for 'tis your voice,' said he.
'Yes.' 'And how many now are living?'
    'Three.' "

CHOICE BETWIXT TWO WAYFARERS

DEATH I beheld, and Shame I saw. The two
At evening went a lonely forest through.
Chill blew the blast, the trees unshapely showed,
And Death upon a dead horse ghastly rode,
And Shame upon a putrid steed rode by;
Of strange black birds you heard the dismal cry.

Said Shame, "In me you happiness behold.
I wend to joy. Come! Purple, silk, and gold;
Feasts, palaces, and priests and jollity;
Triumphant laughter; chambers vast and high;
Riches that bid you take whate'er you please;
Parks; starlit Edens full of stately trees;
Women who haste to meet you, beauty-browed;
Fame placing to his lips his trumpet loud;
Renown and glory sounding far and free—
All this is yours if you will follow me."

"Your horse has an ill odor," I replied.

Death said, "My name is duty, and I ride
Toward the grave through toil and agony."

"And hast thou room behind thee?" answered I.

Since then, toward darkness, where doth God
    appear,
We ride together through the forest drear.

———

CIVIL WAR

FURIOUS and dreadful was the crowd. They
    cried
"To death!" round one who kept his calm cold
    pride
Unmoved, and who himself seemed pitiless—
"Death to the wretch!" The crowd around him
    press.

To him it seemed a thing of course to die;
The game is lost, yours is the victory.
Well, let him die. Where the mob thickest meet,
They drag him from his home into the street.
"Death to the man!" a hundred voices cried;
His garments were with recent slaughter dyed.

This man was one of those who wage blind war
With kings against the people, nor compare
Brutus with Scœvola, Blanqui with Barbès;
He'd killed, no matter whom, the livelong day.

Pity and fear alike to him unknown,
His hands by powder blackened freely shown.
A woman seized his coat. "Here on this spot
Kneel down! A soldier! He our comrades
 shot!"
"True," said the man. "Down with him!—
 Shoot him!—Kill!"
The people shrieked. "Here—There—At the
 Bastile!
To th' Arsenal—Come, march!" "Where you
 like best,"
The captive said. All grim, with ranks close
 prest,
Loaded with guns. 'Let the vile soldier die,
As though a wolf!" The man said quietly,
"'Tis well; I am the wolf, but you're the
 hounds."
"He mocks us!" "Death!" from a hundred
 voices sounds.
Clinched fists assail the haughty captive now,
Whose lips o'erflow with gall, with gloom his
 brow.
Still "Death!" they shout; "we'll have no em-
 peror!"
You saw his eyes contempt and fury pour;
And calm he trampled, full of proud disdain,
O'er corpses which perhaps himself had slain.

Dread are the people when they wild are made;
He, 'neath their taunts, the higher holds his
 head.
They more than hold him—they invade, attack.

God! how they hate him! How he hates them
  back!
How, if the victor, he had shot them all!
"Kill him! Just now he riddled us with ball!
Down with the traitor, the accurs'd, the spy!
Death to the brigand!"—
  They hear suddenly
A little voice, which "'Tis my father," said;
The effect of unexpected light was made.
A child appeared—a child of six years old—
His arms held out in prayer, yet threatening
  bold.

All shouted, "Let the spy be shot, be crushed!"
Then 'twixt the captive's knees the infant
  rushed,
And cried, his brow bright with baptismal
  ray,
"Father, they shall not do you harm, I say!"
The child from the same dwelling-place came
  out.

"Down with him! Death!" increasing clamors
  shout;
"Down with him! Of the murderer make an
  end!"
Cannon and tocsin in the distance blend.
Now men of fearful mien fill all the street;
"Crush minister, priest, king, beneath your
  feet;
Kill all—a lot of bandits, villains, spies!"
"But since I tell you," still the infant cries,
"That he's my father!—"

              "Pretty child!" then said
One woman.—Soul his azure eyes displayed;
Pale, all in tears, he decent clothes had on.
Another said, "Your age, my little one?"
"Don't kill my father!" did the child reply.

Then to the ground sunk many a thoughtful
    eye;
Their hands no more the man so hardly prest.

One more enraged, more ruthless than the
    rest,
Said to the child, "Begone!" "Where?"
    "Home!" "What for?"
"Your mother." Said the father, "She's no
    more."
"Then he has none but you?" the man replied.
"What matters that?" and then himself applied
To warm the little hands that shivered so.
Then to his boy: "Dame Catherine, you know."
"Our neighbor?" "Yes; go to her." "You'll
    come too?"
"Yes, presently." "I won't go without you."
"Why?" "Lest they hurt you."—
                And the father then
Whispered the chief of these infuriate men,
"Leave go my collar, gently lead the way;
I'll tell the child that I'm all safe to-day.
In the next street or elsewhere, at your choice,
You then can shoot me." With a surly voice,
"Well!" said the chief, and let the captive be.
The father then: "We walk as friends, you see,
These gentlemen and I." So after this:

"Be good; go home."   The child then sought a
    kiss,
And went away, quite happy, void of dread.

"And now we're undisturbed," the father said;
"Kill me where'er you please, elsewhere or
    here."

Then in that roar of battle you might hear
A thrill, a murmur, from the crowd to come,
And all the people shouted, "Get you home!"

THE VANISHED CITY

WATER is never idle.   Thousand years,
Ere Adam was, that specter with white hairs,
Our ancestor—so your descent you trace—
When giants still mixed with the human race,
In times whereof Tradition speaketh not,
A brick-built city stood upon the spot
Where now the north wind stirs the ocean foam.
That city was of mad excess the home.
Pale lightnings did at times its riot threat;
What now is sea was a wide plain as yet;
Ships voyage now where chariots rolled before,
And hurricanes replace the kings of yore.
For, to make deserts, God, who rules mankind,
Begins with kings, and ends the work by wind.
This folk, this ant-hill, rumor, gossip, noise,
This troop of souls, by sorrow moved, and joys,
Sounded as in a tempest hums a swarm:
The neighboring ocean caused them no alarm.

This city had its kings—kings proud and great,
Who heads had 'neath them, as the reapers
    wheat,
Were they bad? No. But they were kings.
    And kings
Are men o'er-high, whom a vague terror wrings.
In wrong they pleasure seek and fears allay,
And are, 'mid beasts of burden, beasts of prey.
" 'Tis not their fault!" the sage with pity cries;
"They would be better if born otherwise."
Men still are men. The despot's wickedness
Comes of ill teaching, and of power's excess—
Comes of the purple he from childhood wears.
Slaves would be tyrants if the chance were theirs.

This ancient city, then, was built of brick,
With ships, bazaars, and lofty towers thick;
Arches, and palaces for music famed,
And brazen monsters which their gods they
    named.
Cruel and gay, this town, whose squares and
    streets
Showed gibbets which the crowd with laughter
    greets;
Hymns of forgetfulness they sing, for man
Is but a breath, and only lasts a span.
The avenues by sparkling lakes were closed;
The king's wives bathed, their naked charms
    exposed
In parks where peacocks all their stars display.
Hammers that drive the sleeper's rest away,
Pounded on anvils black, from dawn to night,
And vultures preened their feathers, and alight,

Upon the temples, by no fears deterred
For savage idols love the cruel bird;
Tigers with hydras suit; the eagles know
That they no ancient customs overthrow
If, when blood flows from th' altar to the sod,
They come, and share the slaughter with the god.
Pure gold the altar of that fane august;
The cedar roof was clinched, for fear of rust,
With wooden pegs for nails, and night and day
Did hautboys, clarions, cymbals loudly play
For fear their savage gods should fall asleep.
Such life, such deeds that mighty city steep,
There women flock for riot vile, and pelf.

One day the ocean 'gan to stir itself,
Gently, devoid of rage, beside the town;
It silently gnawed through the rocks, and down,
Without noise, shock, or the least movement
    rough,
Like a grave workman who has time enough.
In vain a man, his ear fixed to the ground,
Had closely listened; he had heard no sound.
The water dumbly, softly wears, destroys.
Over deep silence raves the city's noise;
So that at eve, at Nature's shuddering hour,
When, like an Emir of tyrannic power,
Sirius appears, and on the horizon black
Bids countless stars pursue their mighty track,
The clouds—the only birds that never sleep—
Collected by the winds through heaven's steep,
The moon, the stars, the white-capped hills,
    descry
Houses, domes, pillars, arches, suddenly

With the whole city—people, army, all,
Their king who sang and feasted in his hall,
And had not time to rise up from the board—
Sink, into nameless depth of darkness poured;
And while at once, heaped up from top to base,
Towers, palaces, are 'gulfed without a trace,
A hoarse, a savage murmuring arose,
And you behold like a vast mouth unclose
A hole, whence spouts a stream of foaming
    wrath—
Gulf where the town falls in, the sea comes
    forth.

And then all vanished: waves roll o'er the plain.
Now you see nothing but the deep, wide main,
Stirred by the winds, alone beneath the skies.

Such is the shock of ocean's mysteries!

———

THE INQUISITION

THE DEFENSE OF MOMOTOMBO

The custom of baptizing volcanoes is traced to the ear-
liest times of the conquest. All the craters of Nicaragua
were thus sanctified with the exception of Momotombo,
whence none of the priests commissioned to plant there
the cross ever returned. — SQUIER: *Travels in South
America*

FINDING that earthquakes far too much pre-
    vailed,
The Spanish kings with sacred rites assailed

Volcanic mountains of the New World land,
Baptizing them; and to the priestly hand
They all submitted, saving only one;
But Momotombo would not have it done.
Divers the surpliced priests who — choice of
    Rome—
Essayed to reach the frowning mountain's dome,
Bearing the Sacrament the Church decrees,
With eyes on heaven fixed; but of all these—
And many were they—none were heard of more.

"O Momotombo! thou colossus hoar,
Who ponderest by the sea, while thou hast made
Tiara of thy crater's flame and shade,
Why, when thy dreadful threshold we draw
    near,
And bring thee God, why wilt thou not us hear?"
Stayed was the belching of its lava tide,
While gravely Momotombo thus replied:

"I liked not much the god you chased away;
His jaws were black with gory rot alway.
Eater of human flesh was he, this god,
And miser hiding gold beneath the sod.
His cave, the porch to frightful yard, was made
Sepulchral temple where his pontiff stayed.
The slaughterer deaf, deformed, of hideous mien,
Bleeding between his teeth was ever seen
A corpse, while round his wrists the serpents
    twined,
And horrid skeletons of human kind
Grinn'd at his feet.   Oh, cruel were the ways
Of shocking murder in those dreadful days, .

Blackening the firmament sublime.   At this
I groaned from out the depths of my abyss.
Thus when came proudly o'er the trembling sea
White men, from that side whence unfailingly
The morning ever breaks, it seemed to me
That to receive them well were only wise.
'White men,' said I, 'resemble azure skies;
Surely the color of their souls we trace—
It must be like the color of their face.
The god that these men worship must be good;
Murders will cease,' and I in happy mood
Rejoiced—the ancient priest I hated so.
But when the new one's work began to show,
When I could see the Inquisition flame,
That ne'er was quenched, taking the Holy name,
A mournful torch that to my level reached,
Just Heaven! when thus you daily taught and
        preached,
And Torquemada tried with fiery might
To dissipate the darkness of the night
Of savage heathendom; when I saw then
How he would civilize; at Lima, when
I saw the osier giants, in the strife,
Filled to the brim with childish baby life
Crackling above the mighty furnace heat,
And curls of smoke round burning women meet,
Choked by the stench of every horrid deed—
Auto-da-fe according to your creed—
I, who but shadow brightly burn away,
Repented of my gladness, forced to say,
When looking at the strangers' god more near,
'To change is not worth while, it doth appear!' "

THE SWISS MERCENARIES

When the regiment of Halberdiers
  Is proudly marching by,
The eagle of the mountain screams
  From out his stormy sky;
Who speaketh to the precipice,
  And to the chasm sheer;
Who hovers o'er the thrones of kings,
  And bids the caitiffs fear.
King of the peak and glacier,
  King of the cold, white scalps,
He lifts his head at that close tread,
  The eagle of the Alps.

"Oh, shame! those men that march
    below;
  Oh, ignominy dire!
Are the sons of my free mountains
  Sold for imperial hire.
Ah, the vilest in the dungeon,
  Ah, the slave upon the seas,
Is great, is pure, is glorious,
  Is grand compared with these,
Who, born amid my holy rocks,
  In solemn places high,
Where the tall pines bend like rushes
  When the storm goes sweeping by,

"Yet give the strength of foot they
    learned
  By perilous path and flood,

And from their blue-eyed mothers
  won,
The old, mysterious blood;
The daring that the good south wind
  Into their nostrils blew,
And the proud swelling of the heart
  With each pure breath they drew;
The graces of the mountain glens,
  With flowers in summer gay;
And all the glories of the hills—
  To earn a lackey's pay.

"Their country free and joyous—
  She of the rugged sides,
She of the rough peaks arrogant
  Whereon the tempest rides;
Mother of the unconquered thought
  And of the savage form,
Who brings out of her sturdy heart
  The hero and the storm;
Who giveth freedom unto man,
  And life unto the beast;
Who hears her silver torrents ring
  Like joy-bells at a feast;

"Who hath her caves for palaces,
  And where her châlets stand
The proud old archer of Altorf,
  With his good bow in his hand—
Is she to suckle jailers?
  Shall shame and glory rest,
Amid her lakes and glaciers,
  Like twins upon her breast?

Shall the two-headed eagle,
  Marked with her double blow,
Drink of her milk through all those
      hearts
  Whose blood he bids to flow?

"Say, was it pomp ye needed,
  And all the proud array
Of courtly joust and high parade
  Upon a gala day?
Look up: have not my valleys
  Their torrents white with foam,
Their lines of silver bullion
  On the blue hillocks of home?
Doth not sweet May embroider
  My rocks with pearls and flowers?
Her fingers trace a richer lace
  Than yours in all my bowers.

"Are not my old peaks gilded
  When the sun arises proud,
And each one shakes a white mist
      plume
  Out of the thunder-cloud?
O neighbor of the golden sky,
  Sons of the mountain sod!
Why wear a base king's colors
  For the livery of God?
Oh, shame! despair! to see my Alps
  Their giant shadows fling
Into the very waiting-room
  Of tyrant and of king!

"O thou deep heaven, unsullied yet,
　　Into thy gulfs sublime,
Up azure tracks of flaming light,
　　Let my free pinion climb,
Till from my sight, in that clear light,
　　Earth and her crimes be gone—
The men who act the evil deeds,
　　The caitiffs who look on;
Far, far into that space immense,
　　Beyond the vast white veil
Where distant stars come out and
　　shine,
And the great sun grows pale."

CONSCIENCE

THEN, with his children, clothed in skins of
　　brutes,
Disheveled, livid, rushing through the storm,
Cain fled before Jehovah.   As night fell,
The dark man reached a mount in a great plain;
And his tired wife and his sons, out of breath,
Said, "Let us lie down on the earth and sleep."
Cain, sleeping not, dreamed at the mountain foot.
Raising his head, in that funereal heaven
He saw an Eye—a great Eye, in the night,
Open, and staring at him in the gloom.
"I am too near," he said, and tremblingly woke
　　up
His sleeping sons again, and his tired wife,

And fled through space and darkness.   Thirty
    days
He went, and thirty nights, nor looked behind;
Pale, silent, watchful, shaking at each sound;
No rest, no sleep, till he attained the strand
Where the sea washes that which since was
    Asshur.
"Here pause," he said, "for this place is secure;
Here may we rest, for this is the world's end."
And he sat down; when, lo! in the sad sky,
The self-same Eye on the horizon's verge!
And the wretch shook as in an ague fit.
"Hide me!" he cried; and all his watchful sons,
Their finger on their lip, stared at their sire.
Cain said to Jabal (father of them that dwell
In tents): "Spread here the curtain of thy tent."
And they spread wide the floating canvas roof,
And made it fast, and fixed it down with lead.
"You see naught now," said Zillah then, fair
    child,
The daughter of his eldest, sweet as day.
But Cain replied, "That Eye, I see it still!"
And Jubal cried (the father of all those
That handle harp and organ): "I will build
A sanctuary;" and he made a wall of bronze,
And set his sire behind it.   But Cain moaned,
"That Eye is glaring at me ever!"   Henoch
    cried:
"Then must we make a circle vast of towers,
So terrible that nothing dare draw near.
Build we a city with a citadel;
Build we a city high, and close it fast."
Then Tubal Cain (instructor of all them

That work in brass and iron) built a tower—
Enormous, superhuman. While he wrought,
His fiery brothers from the plain around
Hunted the sons of Enoch and of Seth;
They plucked the eyes out of whoever passed,
And hurled at even arrows to the stars.
They set strong granite for the canvas wall,
And every block was clamped with iron chains:
It seemed a city made for hell. Its towers,
With their huge masses, made night in the land.
The walls were thick as mountains. On the door
They graved, "Let not God enter here." This
    done,
And having finished to cement and build
In a stone tower, they set him in the midst.
To him, still dark and haggard: "Oh, my sire,
Is the Eye gone?" quoth Zillah, tremblingly.
But Cain replied, "Nay, it is even there!"
Then added, "I will live beneath the earth,
As a lone man within his sepulcher.
I will see nothing; will be seen of none."
They digged a trench, and Cain said, " 'Tis
    enow,"
As he went down alone into the vault;
But when he sat, so ghost-like, in his chair,
And they had closed the dungeon o'er his head,
The Eye was in the tomb, and fixed on Cain.

SONG OF THE PROW GILDERS

WE are the gilders of the prows.
Wheel-like awhirl, strong winds arouse
    The verdant sea's rotundity,
Mingling the shadows and the gleams,
And 'mid the folds of somber streams
    Drawing slant vessels steadfastly.

The shrilling squall close-circling flies,
The tortuous winds deep guiles devise,
    The Archer black in his horn doth blow;
These sounds bode death's dark mystery.
And through these prodigies 'tis we
    That make the golden specters go;

For the ship's prow is like a ghost.
Still wave-engirdled, tempest-tost.
    Proudly from our bazaars she sails
To serve the lightnings with a mark,
And midst the hazards of the dark
    To be an eye that never fails.

King, 'neath the plane-trees pleasure thee;
Sultan to the sultanas see,
    And hide beneath long veils the grace
Of myriad girls with names untold
Who yester-morn stark-bare were sold
    By auction on the market-place.

What cares the wave! What cares the air!
This girl is dark and that is fair,
　Of Halep she, or Ispahan;
Before thy face they all may quake.
What heed thereof, forsooth, should take
　The vast mysterious ocean!

Ye have each one your revelry.
Be thou the prince, the tempest he.
　He lightning hath, the yataghan
Thou, to chastise your multitudes;
Beneath its lord the people broods,
　The wave beneath the hurricane.

For one and the other do we strive—
This double task is ours alive;
　And thus we sing: O stern emir,
Thine eyes of steel, thy heart of ice
Keep not the little swallow's eyes
　From trustful sleep when night is near;

For holy Nature is eterne
And tranquil.　Living souls that yearn,
　God sheltereth beneath His wing;
Amid the all-serene sweet shade,
With hearts forever undismayed
　By spectral terrors, do we sing.

Unto our lords we leave the palm
And statelier laurel.　We are calm
　And steadfast while within their hand
They have not ta'en the 'minished stars,
And the swift flight of the cloud-cars
　Depends not on a king's command.

The summer glows, the flowers bloom
    bright,
Small rose-buds tip the bosoms white·
    One hunts, one laughs; the craftsmen still
Sing, and the priests still sigh and sleep·
Slight shadowy fawns, through copses deep
    Fleeing, make greyhounds strain and
    thrill.

If soothly, sultan, thou hadst quaffed
All proffered pleasures, the sweet draught
    Would surely quickly poison thee!
Live thou and reign—thy life is sweet.
Couched on the moss the roebuck fleet
    In forest slumbers dreamfully.

Who mounts aloft must needs descend;
The hours are flame, dust is their end;
    The tomb saith unto man: "Behold!"—
Times change: blithe birds not alway sing;
Waves lisp, and straight are thundering,
    While aye around are omens rolled.

The hour is sultry: women, bare, ·
Lave lovely limbs nigh blooms less fair;
    All lightest sorrows now repose;
O'er blue tranced lakes white clouds are
        driven;
With the most golden star of heaven
    Crowneth itself earth's reddest rose.

Thy gallev we have gold-arrayed
By sixty pairs of oars is swayed,

Which from Lepanto, 'mid the surge,
Subdue the tempest and the tide,
And each of which is hotly plied
By four slaves shackled, 'neath the scourge.

THE BOY-KING'S PRAYER

THE good steed flew o'er river and o'er plain,
Till far away—no need of spur or rein.
The child, half rapture, half solicitude,
Looks back anon, in fear to be pursued;
Shakes lest some raging brother of his sire
Leap from those rocks that o'er the path aspire.

On the rough granite bridge, at evening's fall,
The white horse paused by Compostella's wall.
('Twas good Saint James that reared those
    arches tall.)
Through the dim mist stood out each belfry
    dome,
And the boy hailed the paradise of home.

Close to the bridge, set on high stage, they
    meet
A Christ of stone, the Virgin at his feet.
A taper lighted that dear pardoning face,
More tender in the shade that wrapped the
    place,
And the child stayed his horse, and in the shine
Of the wax taper knelt down at the shrine.

"O my good God! O Mother Maiden sweet!"
He said, "I was the worm beneath men's feet·
My father's brethren held me in their thrall,
But thou didst send the Paladin of Gaul,
O Lord! and show'dst what different spirits
    move
The good men and the evil—those who love
And those who love not. I had been as they,
But thou, O God, hast saved both life and soul
    to-day.
I saw thee in that noble knight; I saw
Pure light, true faith, and honor's sacred law,
My Father, and I learned that monarchs must
Compassionate the weak, and unto all be just.
O Lady Mother! O dear Jesus! thus
Bowed at the cross where Thou didst bleed for
    us,
I swear to hold the truth that now I learn,
Leal to the loyal, to the traitor stern,
And ever just and nobly mild to be,
Meet scholar of that Prince of Chivalry;
And here thy shrine bear witness, Lord, for
    me."

The horse of Roland, hearing the boy tell
His vow, looked round and spoke: "O King, 'tis
    well!"
Then on the charger mounted the child-king,
And rode into the town, while all the bells 'gan
    ring.

AFTER THE BATTLE

My father, hero of benignant mien,
On horseback visited the gory scene,
After the battle as the evening fell,
And took with him a trooper loved right well,
Because of bravery and presence bold.
The field was covered with the dead, all cold,
And shades of night were deepening: came a
    sound,
Feeble and hoarse, from something on the
    ground;
It was a Spaniard of the vanquished force,
Who dragged himself with pain beside their
    course.
Wounded and bleeding, livid and half dead,
"Give me to drink--in pity, drink!" he said.
My father, touched, stretched to his follower
    now
A flask of rum that from his saddle-bow
Hung down: "The poor soul—give him drink,"
    said he.
But while the trooper prompt, obediently
Stooped toward the other, he of Moorish race
Pointed a pistol at my father's face,
And with a savage oath the trigger drew:
The hat flew off, a bullet passing through.
As swerved his charger in a backward stride,
"Give him to drink the same," my father cried.

THE LIONS

FAMISHED the lions were in their strong den,
And roared appeal to Nature from the men
Who caged them—Nature, that for them had
    care.
Kept for three days without their needful fare
The creatures raved with hunger and with hate,
And through their roof of chains and iron grate
Looked to the blood-red sunset in the west;
Their cries the distant traveler oppressed
Far as horizon which the blue hill veils.

Fiercely they lashed their bodies with their
    tails
Till the walls shook, as if their eyes' red light
And hungry jaws had lent them added might.

By Og and his great sons was shaped the cave;
They hollowed it, in need, themselves to save.
It was a deep-laid place wherein to hide
This giant's palace in the rock's dark side;
Their heads had broken through the roof of
    stone,
So that the light in every corner shone,
And dreary dungeon had for dome blue sky.
Nebuchadnezzar, savage king, had eye
For this strong cavern, and a pavement laid
Upon the center, that it should be made
A place where lions he could safely mew,
Though once Deucalions and Khans it knew.

The beasts were four, most furious all. The
    ground
Was carpeted with bones that lay all round;
While as they walked, and crunched with heavy
    tread
Men's skeletons and brutes', far overhead
The tapering shadows of the rocks were spread.

The first had come from Sodom's desert plain;
When savage freedom did to him remain
He dwelt at Sin, extremest point and rude
Of silence terrible and solitude.
Oh! woe betide who fell beneath his claw,
This lion of the sand with rough-skinned paw.

The second came from forest water'd by
The stream Euphrates; when his step drew
    nigh,
Descending to the river, all things feared;
Hard fight to snare this growler it appeared.
The hounds of two kings were employed to
    catch
This lion of the woods and be his match.

The third one dwelt on the steep mountain's
    side,
Horror and gloom companioned every stride;
When toward the miry ravines they would
    stray,
And herds and flocks in their wild gambols
    play,
All fled—the shepherd, warrior, priest—in fright
If he leaped forth in all his dreadful might.

The fourth tremendous, furious creature came
From the seashore, and prowled with leonine
    fame
Before he knew captivity's hard throes,
Along the coast where Gur's strong city rose.
Reeking its roofs, and in its ports were met
The masts of many nations thickly set.
There peasants brought their manna fine, and
    gum,
And there the prophet on his ass would come;
And folks were happy as caged birds set free.

Gur had a market-place 'twas grand to see;
There Abyssinians brought their ivories rare,
And Amorrhiens amber for their ware,
And linens dark. From Asser came fine wheat,
And from famed Ascalon the butter sweet.
The fleet of vessels stir on ocean made.
This beast in reverie of evening's shade
Was fretted by the noisy town so near,
Too many folks lived in it, that was clear.
Gur was a lofty, formidable town;
At night three heavy barriers made it frown
And closed the entrance inaccessible.
Between each battlement rose terrible
Rhinoceros horn, or one of buffalo;
The strong, straight wall did like a hero show.
Some fifteen fathoms deep the moat might be
And it was filled by sluices from the sea.
Instead of kenneled watch-dogs barking near,
Two monstrous dragons did for guards appear—
They had been captured 'mong the reeds of Nile,
And by magician tamed to guards servile.

One night the gate thus kept the lion neared:
With single bound the guarding moat he
 cleared;
Then with barbaric teeth the gate he smashed
And all its triple bars; and next he crashed
The dragons twain, without so much as look
At them; and bolts and hinges all he shook
Into one wreck. And when he made his way
Back toward the strand, remained there of the
 fray
Only a vision of the peopled town,
Only a memory of the wall knocked down,
'Neath spectral towers fit but for vulture's nest,
Or for the tiger wanting timely rest.

This lion scorned complaint, but crouching lay
And yawned, so heavily time passed away
Mastered by man, sharp hunger thus he bore,
Yet weariness of woe oppressed him sore.

But to and fro the others stamp all three,
And if a fluttering bird outside they see,
They gnaw its shadow as they mark it soar,
Their hunger growing as they hoarsely roar.

In a dark corner of the cavern dim
Quite suddenly there oped a portal grim,
And pushed by brawny arms that fright be-
 trayed
Appeared a man in grave clothes white arrayed.

The grating closed as closing up a tomb;
The man was with the lions in the gloom.

The monsters foamed, and rushed their prey to
    gain,
With frightful yell, while bristled every mane,
Their howling roar expressing keenest hate
Of savage nature rebel to its fate,
With anger dashed by fear. Then spoke the
    man,
And stretching forth his hand his words thus
    ran:
"May peace be with you, lions." Paused the
    beasts.

The wolves that disinter the dead for feasts,
The flat-skulled. bears, and writhing jackals,
    they
Who prowl at shipwrecks on the rocks for prey,
Are fierce; hyenas are unpitying found,
And watchful tiger felling at one bound;
But the strong lion in his stately force
Will sometimes lift the paw, yet stay its course.
He the lone dreamer in the shadows gray.
And now the lions grouped themselves; and
    they
Amid the ruins looked like elders set
On grave discussion, in a conclave met,
With knitted brows intent disputes to end,
While over them a dead tree's branches bend.

First spoke the lion of the sandy plain
And said, "When this man entered I again
Beheld the midday sun, and felt the blast
Of the hot simoom blown o'er spaces vast.
Oh, this man from the desert comes, I see!"

Then spoke the hon of the woods: "For me,
One time where fig and palm and cedars grow,
And holly, day and night came music's flow
To fill my joyous cave; even when still
All life, the foliage round me seemed to thrill
With song.   When this man spoke, a sound was
    made
Like that from birds' nests in the mossy shade.
This man has journeyed from my forest home!"

And now the one which had the nearest come,
The lion black from mountains huge exclaimed:
"This man is like to Caucasus, far-famed,
Where no rock stirs; the majesty has he
Of Atlas.   When his arm he raised all free,
I thought that Lebanon had made a bound,
And thrown its shadow vast on fields around.
This man comes to us from the mountain's side!"

The lion dweller near the ocean wide,
Whose roar was loud as roar of frothing sea,
Spoke last.   "My sons, my habit is," said he,
"In sight of grandeur wholly to ignore
All enmity; and this is why the shore
Became my home.   I watched the sun arise
And moon, and the grave smile of dawn; mine
    eyes
Grew used to the sublime.   While waves rolled
    by
I learned great lessons of eternity.
Now, how this man is named, I do not know;
But in his eyes I see the heavens glow.
This man, with brow so calm, by God is sent."

When night had darkened the blue firmament,
The keeper wished to see inside the gate,
And pressed his pale face 'gainst the fastened
    grate.
In the dim depth stood Daniel, calm of mien,
With eyes uplifted to the stars serene;
While this the sight for wondering gaze to
    meet—
The lions fawning at the captive's feet!

———

BOAZ ASLEEP

At work within his barn since very early,
  Fairly tired out with toiling all the day,
  Upon the small bed where he always lay
Boaz was sleeping by his sacks of barley.

Barley and wheat fields he possessed, and well,
  Though rich, loved justice; wherefore all the
    flood
  That turned his mill-wheels was unstained
    with mud,
And in his smithy blazed no fire of hell.

His beard was silver, as in April all
  A stream may be; he did not grudge a
    stook.
  When the poor gleaner passed, with kindly
    look
Quoth he, "Of purpose let some handfuls fall."

He walked his way of life straight on and plain,
  With justice clothed, like linen white and
    clean,
  And ever rustling.   Toward the poor, I ween,
Like public fountains ran his sacks of grain.

Good master, faithful friend, in his estate
  Frugal yet generous, beyond the youth
  He won regard of woman, for in sooth
The young man may be fair: the old man's
    great.   •

Life's primal source, unchangeable and bright,
  The old man entereth, the day eterne;
  And in the young man's eye a flame may
    burn,
But in the old man's eye one seeth light.
  .   .   .   .

As Jacob slept, or Judith, so full deep
  Slept Boaz 'neath the leaves.   Now it betided,
  Heaven's gate being partly open, that there
    glided
A fair dream forth, and hovered o'er his sleep.

And in his dream to heaven, the blue and broad,
  Right from his loins an oak-tree grew amain.
  His race ran up it far, like a long chain;
Below it sung a king, above it died a God.

Whereupon Boaz murmured in his heart,
  "The number of my years is past fourscore:
  How may this be?   I have not any more
Or son, or wife; yea, she who had her part

"In this my couch, O Lord, is now in thine;
And she, half living, I half dead within,
Our beings still commingle and are twin.
It cannot be that I should found a line!

"Youth hath triumphal mornings; its days
        bound
    From night, as from a victory. But such
    A trembling as the birch-tree's to the touch
Of winter is an eld, and evening closes round.
                .

"I bow myself to death, as kine to meet
    The water bow their fronts athirst," he said.
    The cedar feeleth not the rose's head,
Nor he the woman's presence at his feet.

For while he slept, the Moabitess Ruth
    Lay at his feet, expectant of his waking.
    He knowing not what sweet guile she was
        making;
She knowing not what God would have, in sooth.

Asphodel scents did Gilgal's breezes bring;
    Through nuptial shadows, questionless, full
        fast
    The angels sped, for momently there passed
A something blue which seemed to be a wing.

Silent was all in Jezreel and Ur;
    The stars were glittering in the heaven's dusk
        meadows.
    Far west, among those flowers of the shadows,
The thin clear crescent lustrous over her,

Made Ruth raise question, looking through the
 bars
Of heaven, with eyes half-oped, what God,
 what comer
Unto the harvest of the eternal summer,
Had flung his golden hook down on the field of
 stars.

THE PARRICIDE

KING CANUTE died: encoffined he was laid.
Of Aarhuus came the bishop prayers to say,
And sang a hymn upon his tomb, and held
That Canute was a saint—Canute the Great;
That from his memory breathed celestial per-
 fume,
And that they saw him, they the priests, in
 glory,
Seated at God's right hand, a prophet crowned.

       Evening came,
And hushed the organ in the holy place,
And the priests, issuing from the temple doors,
Left the dead king in peace. Then he arose,
Opened his gloomy eyes, and grasped his sword,
And went forth loftily. The massy walls
Yielded before the phantom, like a mist.

There is a sea where Aarhuus, Altona,
And Elsinore's vast domes and shadowy towers
Glass in deep waters. Over this he went
Dark, and still Darkness listened for his foot
Inaudible, itself being but a dream.

Straight to Mount Savo went he, gnawed by
    time,
And thus, "O mountain buffeted of storms,
Give me of thy huge mantle of deep snow
To frame a winding-sheet." The mountain
    knew him,
Nor dared refuse; and with his sword Canute
Cut from its flank white snow, enough to make
The garment he desired, and then he cried,
"Old mountain, Death is dumb, but tell me thou
The way to God." More deep each dread ravine
And hideous hollow yawned, and sadly thus
Answered that hoar associate of the clouds:
"Specter, I know not; I am always here."
Canute departed, and with head erect,
All white and ghastly in his robe of snow,
Went forth into great silence and great night
By Iceland and Norway. After him
Gloom swallowed up the universe. He stood
A sovran kingdomless, a lonely ghost
Confronted with Immensity. He saw
The awful Infinite, at whose portal pale
Lightning sinks dying; Darkness, skeleton
Whose joints are nights; and utter Formlessness
Moving confusedly in the horrible dark,
Inscrutable and blind. No star was there,
Yet something like a haggard gleam; no sound
But the dull tide of Darkness, and her dumb
And fearful shudder. " 'Tis the tomb," he said;
"God is beyond!" Three steps he took, then
    cried—
'Twas deathly as the grave, and not a voice
Responded, nor came any breath to sway

The snowy mantle, with unsullied white
Emboldening the spectral wanderer.
Sudden he marked how, like a gloomy star,
A spot grew broad upon his livid robe.
Slowly it widened, raying darkness forth;
And Canute proved it with his spectral hands
It was a drop of blood.

But he saw nothing; space was black—no sound.
"Forward!" said Canute, raising his proud head.
There fell a second stain beside the first,
Then it grew larger, and the Cimbrian chief
Stared at the thick vague darkness, and saw
    naught.
Still as a bloodhound follows on his track,
Sad he went on. There fell a third red stain
On the white-winding sheet. He had never fled;
Howbeit, Canute forward went no more,
But turned on that side where the sword arm
    hangs:
A drop of blood, as if athwart a dream,
Fell on the shroud, and reddened his right hand.
Then, as in reading one turns back a page,
A second time he changed his course, and turned
To the dim left: there fell a drop of blood.
Canute drew back, trembling to be alone,
And wished he had not left his burial couch.
But when a blood-drop fell again, he stopped,
Stooped his pale head, and tried to make a prayer.
Then fell a drop, and the prayer died away
In savage terror. Darkly he moved on,
A hideous specter, hesitating, white,
And ever as he went, a drop of blood

Implacably from the darkness broke away
And stained that awful whiteness. He beheld,
Shaking as doth a poplar in the wind,
Those stains grow darker and more numerous:
Another, and another, and another.
They seemed to light up that funereal gloom,
And mingling in the folds of that white sheet,
Made it a cloud of blood. He went, and went
And still from that unfathomable vault
The red blood dropped upon him drop by drop,
Always, forever—without noise, as though
From the black feet of some night-gibbeted
    corpse.
Alas! Who wept those formidable tears?
The Infinite! Toward heaven, of the good
Attainable, through the wild sea of night
That hath not ebb nor flow, Canute went on,
And ever walking, came to a closed door,
That from beneath showed a mysterious light.
Then he looked down upon his winding-sheet,
For that was the great place, the sacred place;
That was a portion of the light of God.
And from behind that door hosannas rang.
The winding sheet was red, and Canute stopped.

This is why Canute from the light of day
Draws ever back, and hath not dared appear
Before the Judge whose face is as the sun;
This is why still remaineth the dark king
Out in the night, and never having power
To bring his robe back to its first pure state,
But feeling at each step a blood-drop fall,
Wanders eternally 'neath the vast black heaven.

EVIRADNUS, THE KNIGHT ERRANT

THE ADVENTURER SETS OUT

WHAT was it Sigismond and Ladisläus said?

I know not if the rock, or tree o'erhead,
Had heard their speech; but when the two
    spake low
Among the trees, a shudder seemed to go·
Through all their branches, just as if that way
A beast had passed to trouble and dismay.
Darker the shadow of the rock was seen,
And then a morsel of the shade between
The somber trees took shape, as it would seem
Some specter walking in the sunset's gleam.

'Tis not a monster rising from its lair,
Nor phantom of the foliage and the air,
'Tis not a morsel of the granite's shade
That walks in deepest hollows of the glade.
'Tis not a vampire nor a specter pale,
But living man, in rugged coat of mail.
It is Alsatia's noble Chevalier,
Eviradnus the Brave, that now is here.

The men who spoke he recognized the while
He rested in the thicket; words of guile
Most horrible were theirs as they passed on,
And to the ears of Eviradnus one,

One word had come which roused him. Well
    he knew
The land which lately he had journeyed through.

He down the valley went unto the inn
Where he had left his horse and page, Gasclin.
The horse had wanted drink, and lost a shoe;
And now, "Be quick!" he said, "with what
    you do,
For business calls me; I must not delay."
He strides the saddle and he rides away.

II

EVIRADNUS

Eviradnus was growing old apace;
The weight of years had left its hoary trace,
But still of knights the most renowned was he,
Model of bravery and purity.
His blood he spared not; ready day or night
To punish crime, his dauntless sword shone bright
In his unblemished hand; holy and white
And loyal all his noble life had been—
A Christian Samson coming on the scene.
With fist alone the gate he battered down
Of Sickingen in flames, and saved the town.
'Twas he, indignant at the honor paid
To crime, who with his heel an onslaught made
Upon Duke Lupus' shameful monument,
Tore down the statue he to fragments rent;
Then column of the Strasburg monster bore
To bridge of Wasselonne, and threw it o'er
Into the waters deep. The people round
Blazon the noble deeds that so abound

From Altorf unto Chaux-de-Fonds, and say,
When he rests musing in a dreamy way,
"Behold, 'tis Charlemagne!"   Tawny to see
And hairy, and seven feet high was he,
Like John of Bourbon.   Roaming hill or wood
He looked a wolf endeavoring to do good.
Bound up in duty, he of naught complained,
The cry for help his aid at once obtained.
Only he mourned the baseness of mankind,
And—that the beds too short he e'er must find.
When people suffer under cruel kings,
With pity moved, he to them succor brings.
'Twas he defended Alix from her foes
As sword of Urraca.   He ever shows
His strength is for the feeble and oppressed;
Father of orphans he, and all distressed.
Kings of the Rhine in strongholds were by
      him
Boldly attacked, and tyrant barons grim.
He freed the towns, defying in his lair
Hugo the Eagle; boldly did he dare
To break the collar of Saverne, the ring
Of Colmar, and the iron torture-thing
Of Schlestadt, and the chain that Haguenau
      bore.
Confront with evil, he an aspect wore
Good but most terrible.   In the dread scale
Which princes weighted with their horrid tale
Of craft and violence, and blood and ill,
And fire and shocking deeds, his sword was
      still
God's counterpoise displayed; ever alert
More evil from the wretched to avert,

Those hapless ones who 'neath heaven's vault at
    night
Raise suppliant hands. His lance loved not the
    plight
Of mouldering in the rack, of no avail;
His battle-ax slipped from supporting nail
Quite easily. 'Twas ill for action base
To come so near that he the thing could trace.
The steel-clad champion death drops all around
As glaciers water. Hero ever found
Eviradnus is kinsman of the race
Of Amadys of Gaul, and knights of Thrace.
He smiles at age. For he who never asked
For quarter from mankind, shall he be tasked
To beg of Time for mercy? Rather he
Would girdle up his loins, like Baldwin be.
Aged he is, but of a lineage rare;
The least intrepid of the birds that dare
Is not the eagle barbed. What matters age?
The years but fire him with a holy rage.
Though late from Palestine, he is not spent;
With age he wrestles, firm in his intent.

III

IN THE FOREST

If in the wood a traveler there had been
That eve, had lost himself, strange sight he'd
    seen.
Quite in the forest's heart a lighted space
Arose to view; in that deserted place
A lone, abandoned hall, with light aglow,
The long neglect of centuries did show.

The castle-towers of Corbus in decay
Were girt by weeds and growths that had their
　　way;
Couch-grass and ivy, and wild eglantine
In subtle scaling warfare all combine.
Subject to such attacks three hundred years,
The donjon yields, and ruin now appears.
E'en as by leprosy the wild boars die,
In moat the crumbled battlements now lie;
Around the snake-like bramble twists its rings;
Freebooter sparrows come on daring wings
To perch upon the swivel-gun, nor heed
Its murmuring growl when pecking in their
　　greed
The mulberries ripe.　With insolence the thorn
Thrives on the desolation so forlorn.
But winter brings revenges; then the Keep
Wakes all vindictive from its seeming sleep,
Hurls down the heavy rain, night after night,
Thanking the season's all-resistless might;
And, when the gutters choke, its gargoyles
　　four
From granite mouths in anger spit and pour
Upon the hated ivy hour by hour.

As to the sword rust is, so lichens are
To towering citadel with which they war.
Alas, for Corbus! dreary, desolate;
And yet its woes the winters mitigate.
It rears itself among convulsive throes
That shake its ruins when the tempest blows.
Winter, the savage warrior, pleases well
With its storm-clouds the mighty citadel.

Restoring it to life. The lightning flash
Strikes like a thief and flies; the winds that
    crash
Sound like a clarion, for the Tempest bluff
Is Battle's sister. And when wild and rough,
The north wind blows, the tower exultant cries,
"Behold me!" When hail-hurling gales arise
Of blustering Equinox, to fan the strife,
It stands erect, with martial ardor rife,
A joyous soldier! When like yelping hound
Pursued by wolves, November comes to bound
In joy from rock to rock, like answering cheer
To howling January now so near,
"Come on!" the Donjon cries to blasts o'er-
    head—
It has seen Attila, and knows not dread.
Oh, dismal nights of contest in the rain
And mist, that furious would the battle gain!
The tower braves all, though angry skies pour
    fast
The flowing torrents, river-like and vast.
From their eight pinnacles the gorgons bay,
And scattered monsters, in their stony way,
Are growling heard; the rampart lions gnaw
The misty air and slush with granite maw;
The sleet upon the griffins spits, and all
The saurian monsters, answering to the squall,
Flap wings; while through the broken ceiling
    fall
Torrents of rain upon the forms beneath,
Dragons and snaked Medusas gnashing teeth
In the dismantled rooms. Like armored knight
The granite castle fights with all its might,

Resisting through the winter. All in vain
The heaven's bluster, January's rain,
And those dread elemental powers we call
The Infinite—the whirlwinds that appall
Thunder and waterspouts — and winds that
    shake
As 'twere a tree its ripened fruit to take.
The winds grow wearied, warring with the
    tower,
The noisy North is out of breath, nor power
Has any blast old Corbus to defeat.
It still has strength their onslaughts worst to
    meet.
Thus, spite of briers and thistles, the old tower
Remains triumphant through the darkest hour.
Superb as pontiff, in the forest shown,
Its rows of battlements make triple crown;
At eve, its silhouette is finely traced
Immense and black, showing the keep is placed
On rocky throne, sublime and high. East,
    west,
And north and south, at corners four, there
    rest
Four mounts—Aptar, where flourishes the pine;
And Toxis, where the elms grow green and fine;
Crobius and Bleyda, giants in their might,
Against the stormy winds to stand and fight;
And these above its diadem uphold
Night's living canopy of clouds unrolled.

The herdsman fears, and thinks its shadow
    creeps
To follow him; and superstition keeps

Such hold that Corbus as a terror reigns.
Folks say the fort a target still remains
For the Black Archer, and that it contains
The cave where the Great Sleeper still sleeps
    sound.
The country people all the castle round
Are frightened easily, for legends grow
And mix with phantoms of the mind.   We
    know
The hearth is cradle of such fantasies,
And in the smoke the cotter sees arise
From low-thatched hut he traces cause of dread;
Thus rendering thanks that he is lowly bred,
Because from such none look for valorous deeds.
The peasant flies the tower, although it leads
A noble knight to seek adventure there,
And, from his point of honor, dangers dare.

Thus very rarely passer-by is seen;
But—it might be with twenty years between,
Or haply less—at unfixed interval
There would a semblance be of festival.
A seneschal and usher would appear,
And troops of servants many baskets bear.
Then were in mystery preparations made,
And they departed; for till night none stayed.
But 'twixt the branches gazers could descry
The blackened hall lit up most brilliantly.
None dared approach, and this the reason why.

IV

THE CUSTOM OF LUSACE

When died a noble Marquis of Lusace,
'Twas custom for the heir who filled his place
Before assuming princely pomp and power
To sup one night in Corbus' olden tower.
From this weird meal he passed to the degree
Of prince and margrave; nor could ever he
Be thought brave knight, or she—if woman
    claim
The rank—be reckoned of unblemished fame
Till they had breathed the air of ages gone,
The funeral odors, in the nest alone
Of its dead masters. Ancient was the race:
To climb the upward stem of proud Lusace
Gives one a vertigo; descended they
From ancestor of Attila, men say.
Their race to him—through Pagans— they trace
    back;
Becoming Christians, they their line could track
Through Lechus, Plato, Otho, to combine
With Ursus, Stephen, in a lordly line.
Of all those masters of the country round
That were on Northern Europe's boundary
    found
(At first were waves, and then the dikes were
    reared),
Corbus in double majesty appeared,
Castle on hill and town upon the plain;
And one who mounted on the tower could gain

A view beyond the pines and rocks, of spires
That pierce the shade the distant scene acquires.
A walled town is it, but 'tis not ally
Of the old citadel's proud majesty;
Unto itself belonging this remained.
Often a castle was thus self-sustained
And equaled towns; witness in Lombardy
Crama, and Prato in fair Tuscany,
And in Apulia Barletta too; each one
Was powerful as a town, and dreaded none.
Corbus ranked thus; its precincts seemed to
    hold
The reflex of its mighty kings of old;
Their great events had witness in these walls,
Their marriages were here and funerals,
And mostly here it was that they were born;
And here crowned barons ruled with pride and
    scorn;
Cradle of Scythian majesty this place.
Now, each new master of this ancient race
A duty owed to ancestors which he
Was bound to carry on. The law's decree
It was that he should pass alone the night
Which made him king, as in their solemn sight.
Just at the forest's edge a clerk was met
With wine in sacred cup and purpose set—
A wine mysterious, which the heir must drink
To cause deep slumber till the day's soft brink.
Then to the castle tower he wends his way,
And finds a supper laid with rich display.
He sups and sleeps, when to his slumbering
    eyes
The shades of kings from Bela all arise.

None dare the tower to enter on this night,
But when the morning dawns, crowds are in
    sight
The dreamer to deliver, whom half dazed,
And with the visions of the night amazed,
They to the old church take, where rests the
    dust
Of Borivorus; then the bishop must,
With fervent blessings on his eyes and mouth,
Put in his hands the stony hatchets both,
With which—even like death impartially—
Struck Attila, with one arm dexterously
The south, and with the other arm the north.

This day the town the threatening flag set forth
Of Marquis Swantibore, the monster he
Who in the wood tied up his wife to be
Devoured by wolves, together with the bull
Of which with jealousy his heart was full.

Even when woman took the place of heir
The tower of Corbus claimed the supper there—
'Twas law; the woman trembled, but must dare.

V

THE MARCHIONESS MAHAUD

Niece of the Marquis—John the Striker named—
Mahaud to-day the marquisate has claimed.
A noble dame, the crown is hers by right;
As woman, she has graces that delight.
A queen devoid of beauty is not queen;
She needs the royalty of beauty's mien.

God in His harmony has equal ends
For cedar that resists and reed that bends;
And good it is a woman sometimes rules,
Holds in her hand the power, and manners
    schools,
And laws and mind; succeeding master proud,
With gentle voice and smile she leads the crowd,
The somber human troop. But sweet Mahand
On evil days had fallen; gentle, good,
Alas! she held the scepter like a flower
Timid yet gay, imprudent for the hour,
And careless too. With Europe all in throes,
Though twenty years she now already knows,
She has refused to marry, although oft
Entreated. It is time an arm less soft
Than hers—a manly arm—supported her;
Like to the rainbow she, one might aver,
Shining on high between the cloud and rain,
Or like the ewe that gambols on the plain
Between the bear and tiger. Innocent,
She has two neighbors of most foul intent;
For foes the beauty has, in life's pure spring—
The German Emperor and the Polish King.

VI

THE TWO NEIGHBORS

The difference this betwixt the evil pair,
Faithless to God, for laws without a care:
One was the claw, the other one the will
Controlling   Yet to Mass they both went still
And on the rosary told their beads each day;
But none the less the world believed that they

Unto the powers of hell their souls had sold.
Even in whispers men each other told
The details of the pact which they had signed
With that dark power, the foe of human kind;
In whispers, for the crowd had mortal dread
Of them so high, and woes that they had spread.
One might be vengeance and the other hate,
Yet lived they side by side, in powerful state
And close alliance. All the people near
From red horizon dwelt in abject fear,
Mastered by them; their figures darkly grand
Had ruddy reflex from the wasted land,
And fires, and towns they sacked. Besides, the
    one,
Like David, poet was; the other shone
As fine musician. Rumor spread their fame,
Declaring them divine, until each name
In Italy's fine sonnets met with praise.
The ancient hierarch in those old days
Had custom strange—a now forgotten thing:
It was a European plan that King
Of France was marquis, and th' imperial head
Of Germany was duke; there was no need
To class the other kings—but barons they,
Obedient vassals unto Rome, their stay.
The King of Poland was but simple knight,
Yet now, for once, had strange unwonted right,
And, as exception to the common state,
This one Samartian King was held as great
As German Emperor; and each knew how
His evil part to play, nor mercv show.
The German had one aim—it was to take
All land he could, and it his own to make.

The Pole already having Baltic shore,
Seized Celtic ports, still needing more and more.
On all the Northern Sea his crafts roused fear;
Iceland beheld his demon navy near.
Antwerp the German burnt, and Prussias twain
Bowed to his yoke. The Polish King was fain
To help the Russian Spotocus—his aid
Was like the help that in their common trade
A sturdy butcher gives a weaker one.
The King it is who seizes; and this done,
The Emperor pillages, usurping right
In war Teutonic, settled but by might.
The King in Jutland cynic footing gains,
The weak coerced, the while with cunning pains
The strong are duped. But 'tis a law they make
That their accord themselves should never break.
From Arctic seas to cities Transalpine
Their hideous talons, curved for sure rapine,
Scrape o'er and o'er the mournful continent;
Their plans succeed, and each is well content.
Thus under Satan's all-paternal care
They brothers are, this royal bandit pair.
Oh, noxious conquerors! with transient rule
Chimera heads; ambition can but fool.
Their misty minds but harbor rottenness,
Loathsome and fetid, and all barrenness;
Their deeds to ashes turn; and, hydra-bred,
The mystic skeleton is theirs to dread.

The daring German and the cunning Pole
Noted to-day a woman had control
Of lands, and watched Mahaud like evil spies;
And from the emp'ror's cruel mouth, with dyes

Of wrath empurpled, came these words of late:
"The empire wearies of the wallet weight
Hung at its back—this High and Low Lusace,
Whose hateful load grows heavier apace
That now a woman holds its ruler's place."
Threatening and blood-suggesting every word.
The watchful Pole was silent, but he heard.

Two monstrous dangers; but the heedless one
Babbles and smiles, and bids all care begone,
Likes lively speech; while all the poor she
    makes
To love her, and the taxes off she takes.
A life of dance and pleasure she has known—
A woman always; in her jeweled crown
It is the pearl she loves, not cutting gems,
For these can wound, and mark men's diadems.
She pays the hire of Homer's copyists,
And in the Courts of Love presiding, lists.

Quite recently unto her court have come
Two men—unknown their names or native home,
Their rank or race; but one plays well the lute,
The other is a troubadour. Both suit
The taste of Mahaud, when on summer eve,
'Neath opened windows, they obtain her leave
To sing upon the terrace, and relate
The charming tales that do with music mate.
In August the Moravians have their fête,
But it is radiant June in which Lusace
Must consecrate her noble margrave race.
Thus in the weird and old ancestral tower
For Mahaud now has come the fateful hour—

The lonely supper which her state decrees.
What matters this to flowers and birds and trees
And clouds and fountains? That the people may
Still bear their yoke, have kings to rule alway?
The water flows, the wind in passing by
In murmuring tones takes up the questioning
    cry.

VII

THE BANQUET-HALL

The old stupendous hall has but one door,
And in the dusk it seems that more and more
The walls recede in space unlimited.
At the far end there is a table spread
That in the dreary void with splendor shines;
For ceiling we behold but rafter lines.
The table is arranged for one sole guest;
A solitary chair doth near it rest,
Throne-like, 'neath canopy that droopeth down
From the black beams; upon the walls are
    shown
The painted histories of the olden might,
The Wendish King Thassilo's sturdy fight
On land with Nimrod, and on ocean wide
With Neptune. Rivers too personified
Appear—the Rhine as by the Meuse betrayed;
And fading groups of Odin in the shade,
And the wolf Fenrir and the Asgard snake.
One might the place for dragons' stable take.
The only lights that in the shed appear
Spring from the table's giant chandelier
With seven iron branches—brought from hell
By Attila Archangel, people tell,

When he had conquered Mammon; and they
 say
That seven souls were the first flames that day
This banquet-hall looks an abyss outlined
With shadowy vagueness, though indeed we find
In the far depth upon the table spread
A sudden, strong, and glaring light is shed,
Striking upon the goldsmith's burnished works,
And on the pheasants killed by traitor hawks.
Loaded the table is with viands cold,
Ewers and flagons, all enough of old
To make a love feast. All the napery
Was Friesland's famous make; and fair to see
The dishes, silver-gilt, and bordered round
With flowers; for fruit, here strawberries were
 found
And citrons, apples too, and nectarines.
The wooden bowls were carved in cunning lines
By peasants of the Murg, whose skillful hands
With patient toil reclaim the barren lands
And make their gardens flourish on a rock,
Or mountain where we see the hunters flock.
A golden cup, with handles Florentine,
Shows horned Acteons, armed and booted fine,
Who fight with sword in hand against the
 hounds.
Roses and gladioles make up bright mounds
Of flowers, with juniper and aniseed;
While sage, all newly cut for this great need,
Covers the Persian carpet that is spread
Beneath the table, and so helps to shed
Around a perfume of the balmy spring.
Beyond is desolation withering.

One hears within the hollow dreary space
Across the grove, made fresh by summer's
    grace,
The wind that ever is with mystic might
A spirit ripple of the Infinite.
The glass restored to frames to creak is made
By blustering wind that comes from neighbor-
    ing glade.
Strange, in this dream-like place, so drear and
    lone,
The guest expected was a living one!
The seven lights from seven arms make glow
Almost with life the staring eyes that show
On the dim frescoes; and along the walls
Is here and there a stool, or the light falls
O'er some long chest, with likeness to a tomb;
Yet were displayed amid the mournful gloom
Some copper vessels, and some crockery ware.
The door—as if it must, yet scarcely dare—
Had opened widely to the night's fresh air.

No voice is heard, for man has fled the place;
But Terror crouches in the corners' space,
And waits the coming guest. This banquet-hall
Of Titans is so high, that he who shall
With wandering eye look up from beam to beam
Of the confused wild roof will haply seem
To wonder that the stars he sees not there.
Giants the spiders are, that weave with care
Their hideous webs, which float the joists amid—
Joists whose dark ends in griffins' jaws are hid.
The light is lurid, and the air like death,
And dark and foul. Even Night holds its breath

A while. One might suppose the door had fear
To move its double leaves, their noise to hear.

VIII

WHAT MORE WAS TO BE SEEN

But the great hall of generations dead
Has something more sepulchral and more dread
Than lurid glare from seven-branched chandelier
Or table lone with stately dais near—
Two rows of arches o'er a colonnade
With knights on horseback all in mail arrayed,
Each one disposed with pillar at his back
And to another vis-à-vis. Nor lack
The fittings all complete: in each right hand
A lance is seen; the armored horses stand
With chamfrons laced, and harness buckled
        sure;
The cuissarts' studs are by their clamps secure;
The dirks stand out upon the saddle-bow;
Even unto the horses' feet do flow
Caparisons; the leather all well clasped,
The gorget and the.spurs with bronze tongues
        hasped;
The shining long sword from the saddle hung,
The battle-ax across the back was flung.
Under the arm a trusty dagger rests,
Each spiked knee-piece its murderous power
        attests.
Feet press the stirrups, hands on bridle shown,
Proclaim all ready, with the visors down;
And yet they stir not, nor is audible
A sound to make the sight less terrible.

Each monstrous horse a frontal horn doth bear.
If e'er the Prince of Darkness herdsman were
These cattle black were his by surest right,
Like things but seen in horrid dreams of night.
The steeds are swathed in trappings manifold,
The armèd knights are grave and stern and cold,
Terrific too; the clinch'd fists seem to hold
Some frightful missive, which the phantom
    hands
Would show if opened out at Hell's commands.
The dusk exaggerates their giant size;
The shade is awed, the pillars coldly rise.
O Night! why are these awful warriors here?

Horses and horsemen that make gazers fear
Are only empty armor; but erect
And haughty mien they all affect
And threatening air, though shades of iron still.
Are they strange larvæ, these their statues ill?
No.   They are dreams of horror clothed in brass,
Which from profoundest depths of evil pass
With futile aim to dare the Infinite!
Souls tremble at the silent specter sight,
As if in this mysterious cavalcade
They saw the weird and mystic halt was made
Of them who at the coming dawn of day
Would fade, and from their vision pass away.
A stranger looking in, these masks to see,
Might deem from Death some mandate there
    might be
At times to burst the tombs, the dead to wear
A human shape, and mustering ranks appear
Of phantoms, each confronting other shade.

Grave-clothes are not more grim and somber
    made
Than are these helms; the deaf and sealed-up
    graves
Are not more icy than these arms; the staves
Of hideous biers have not their joints more strong
Than are the joinings of these legs; the long
Scaled gauntlet fingers look like worms that
    shine,
And battle robes to shroud-like folds incline.
The heads are skull-like, and the stony feet
Seem for the charnel-house but only meet.
The pikes have death's-heads carved, and seem
    to be
Too heavy; but the shapes defiantly
Sit proudly in the saddle, and perforce
The rider looks united to the horse,
Upon whose flanks the mail and harness cross.
The cap of marquis beams near ducal wreath,
And on the helm and gleaming shield beneath
Alternate triple pearls with leaves displayed
Of parsley; and the royal robes are made
So large that with the knightly hauberk they
Seem to o'erspread the palfrey every way.
To Rome the oldest armor might be traced;
And men and horses' armor interlaced,
Blent horribly—the man and steed we feel
Made but one hydra with its scales of steel.

Yet is there history here. Each coat of mail
Is representant of some stirring tale.
Each delta-shaped escutcheon shines to show
A vision of the chief by it we know.

Here are the blood-stained dukes' and marquis'
    line—
Barbaric lords, who amid war's rapine
Bore gilded saints upon their banners still,
Painted on fishes' skin with cunning skill.
Here Geth, who to the slaves cried, "Onward
    go!"
And Mundiaque and Ottocar, Plato
And Ladislaus Kunne; and Welf who bore
These words upon his shield his foes before,
"Nothing there is I fear"; Otho, blear-eyed,
Zultan and Nazamustus, and beside
The later Spignus, e'en to Spartibor
Of triple vision, and yet more and more,
As if a pause at every age were made,
And Antæus' fearful dynasty portrayed.

What do they here so rigid and erect?
What wait they for, and what do they expect?
Blindness fills up the helm 'neath iron brows;
Like sapless tree, no soul the hero knows.
Darkness is now where eyes with flame were
    fraught,
And pierced visor serves for mask of naught.
Of empty void is spectral gaint made,
And each of these all-powerful knights dis-
    played
Is only rind of pride and murderous sin;
Themselves are held the icy grave within.
Rust eats the casques enamored once so much
Of death and daring, which knew kiss-like touch
Of banner—mistress so august and dear;
But not an arm can stir its hinges here.

Behold! how mute are they whose threats were
    heard
Like savage roar, whose gnashing teeth and
    word
Deadened the clarion's tones; the helmets dread
Have not a sound, and all the armor spread;
The hauberks, that strong breathing seemed to
    sway,
Are stranded now in helplessness alway
To see the shadows, still prolonged, that seem
To take at night the image of a dream.
These two great files reach from the door afar
To where the table and the daïs are,
Leaving between their fronts a narrow lane.
On the left side the marquises maintain
Their place, but the right side the dukes retain;
And till the roof, embattled by Spignus,
But worn by time that even that subdues,
Shall fall upon their heads, these forms will
    stand
The grades confronting, one on either hand.
While in advance beyond, with haughty head,
As if commander of this squadron dread,
All waiting signal of the Judgment Day,
In stone was seen in olden sculptors' way
Charlemagne the King, who on the earth had
    found
Only twelve knights to grace his Table Round.

The crests were an assembly of strange things—
Of horrors such as nightmare only brings;
Asps, and spread eagles without beak or feet,
Sirens and mermaids here and dragons meet,

And antlered stags and fabled unicorn,
And fearful things of monstrous fancy born.
Upon the rigid form of morion's sheen
Winged lions and the Cerberus are seen,
And serpents winged and finned—things made
　　to fright
The timid foe alone by sense of sight.
Some leaning forward and the others back,
They looked a growing forest that did lack
No form of terror; but these things of dread
That once on barons' helms the battle led
Beneath the giant banners, now are still,
As if they gaped and found the time but ill,
Wearied the ages passed so slowly by,
And that the gory dead no more did lie
Beneath their feet; pined for the battle-cry,
The　trumpet's　clash,　the　carnage,　and　the
　　strife,
Yawning to taste again their dreadful life.
Like tears upon the palfreys' muzzles were
The hard reflections of the metal there.
From out these specters, ages past exhumed,
And as their shadows on the roof-beams loomed
Cast by the trembling light, each figure wan
Seemed growing, and a monstrous shape to don;
So that the double range of horrors made
The darkened zenith clouds of blackest shade,
That shaped themselves to profiles terrible.

All motionless the coursers horrible,
That formed a legion lured by Death to war.
These men and horses masked, how dread they
　　are!

Absorbed in shadows of the eternal shore,
Among the living all their tasks are o'er.
Silent, they seem all mystery to brave—
These sphinxes whom no beacon light can save—
Upon the threshold of the gulf so near,
As if they faced the great enigma here;
Ready with hoofs between the pillars blue
To strike out sparks, and combats to renew,
Choosing for battlefield the shades below,
Which they provoked by deeds we cannot know,
In that dark realm thought dares not to expound,
False masks from heaven lowered to depths
    profound.

IX

A NOISE ON THE FLOOR

This is the scene on which now enters in
Eviradnus, and follows page Gasclin.
The outer walls were almost all decayed;
The door, for ancient marquises once made—
Raised many steps above the courtyard near—
Commanded view of the horizon clear.
The forest looked a great gulf all around,
And on the rock of Corbus there were found
Secret and blood-stained precipices tall.
Duke Plato built the tower and banquet-hall
Over great pits—so was it Rumor said.
The flooring sounds 'neath Eviradnus' tread
Above abysses many.
                    "Page," said he,
"Come here! Your eyes than mine can better
    see,

For sight is woman-like and shuns the old.
(Ah! he can see enough, when years are told,
Who backward looks.)   But, boy, turn toward
     the glade
And tell me what you see."
                          The boy obeyed,
And leaned across the threshold, while the bright,
Full moon shed o'er the glade its white, pure
     light.

"I see a horse and woman on it now,"
Said Gasclin, "and companions also show."
"Who are they?" asked the seeker of sublime
Adventures.
               "Sir, I now can hear like chime
The sound of voices—and men's voices too
Laughter and talk   Two men there are in view;
Across the road the shadows clear I mark
Of horses three."
                   "Enough.   Now, Gasclin, hark!"
Exclaimed the knight; "you must at once return
By other path than that which you discern,
So that you be not seen.   At break of day
Bring back our horses fresh, and every way
Caparisoned; now leave me, boy, I say."
The page looked at his master like a son,
And said to him, "Oh, if I might stay on,
For they are two."
                    "Go; I suffice alone!"

X
EVIRADNUS MOTIONLESS

And lone the hero is within the hall,
And nears the table where the glasses all
Show in profusion; all the vessels there,
Goblets and glasses gilt, or painted fair,
Are ranged for different wines with practiced
    care.
He thirsts: the flagons tempt; but there must
    stay
One drop in emptied glass, and 'twould betray
The fact that some one living had been here.
Straight to the horses goes he, pauses near
That which is next the table shining bright,
Seizes the rider, plucks the phantom knight
To pieces—all in vain its panoply
And pallid shining to his practiced eye;
Then he conveys the severed iron remains
To corner of the hall where darkness reigns.
Against the wall he lays the armor low
In dust and gloom, like hero vanquished now;
But keeping pond'rous lance and shield so old,
Mounts to the empty saddle, and behold!
A statue Eviradnus has become,
Like to the others in their frigid home.
With visor down, scarce breathing seemed main-
    tained,

Throughout the hall a death-like silence reigned.

XI
A LITTLE MUSIC

Listen! like hum from unseen nests we hear
A mirthful buzz of voices coming near,
Of footsteps, laughter, from the trembling trees.
And now the thick-set forest all receives
A flood of moonlight, and there gently floats
The sound of a guitar of Innsbruck—notes
Which blend with chimes, vibrating to the hand,
Of tiny bell; where sounds a grain of sand.
A man's voice mixes with the melody,
And vaguely melts to song in harmony.

"If you like we'll dream a dream:
    Let us mount on palfreys two;
  Birds are singing: let it seem
    You lure me—and I take you.

"Let us start—'tis eve, you see;
    I'm thy master and thy prey.
  My bright steed shall pleasure be;
    Yours, it shall be love, I say.

"Journeying leisurely we go;
    We will make our steeds touch
        heads,
  Kiss for fodder—and we so
    Satisfy our horses' needs.

"Come! the two delusive things
    Stamp impatiently it seems.
  Yours has heavenward soaring
        wings;
    Mine is of the land of dreams.

"What's our baggage?   Only vows,
    Happiness, and all our care,
And the flower that sweetly shows
    Nestling lightly in your hair.

"Come! the oaks all dark appear,
    Twilight now will soon depart;
Railing sparrows laugh to hear
    Chains thou puttest round my
        heart.

"Not my fault 'twill surely be
    If the hills should vocal prove,
And the trees when us they see,
    All should murmur, 'Let us
        love!'

"Oh, be gentle!   I am dazed.
    See, the dew is on the grass;
Wakened butterflies amazed
    Follow thee as on we pass.

"Envious night-birds open wide
    Their round eyes to gaze a while;
Nymphs that lean their urns beside
    From their grottoes softly smile,

"And exclaim, by fancy stirred,
    'Hero and Leander they;
We in listening for a word
    Let our water fall away.'

"Let us journey Austrian way,
    With the daybreak on our brow;
I be great, and you I say
    Rich, because we love shall know.

"Let us over countries rove,
    On our charming steeds content,
In the azure light of love,
    And its sweet bewilderment.

"For the charges at our inn,
    You with maiden smiles shall
        pay;
    I the landlord's heart will win
    In a scholar's pleasant way.

"You great lady, and I Count—
    Come, my heart has opened quite.
We this tale will still recount
    To the stars that shine at night."

The melody went on some moments more
Among the trees the calm moon glistened o'er,
Then trembled and was hushed; the voice's
    thrill
Stopped like alighting birds, and all was still.

XII

GREAT JOSS AND LITTLE ZENO

Quite suddenly there showed across the door
Three heads, which all a festive aspect wore.
Two men were there; and, dressed in cloth-of-
    gold,
A woman.   Of the men one might have told
Some thirty years; the other younger seemed,
Was tall and fair, and from his shoulder gleamed
A gay guitar with ivy leaves enlaced.
The other man was dark, but pallid-faced

And small. At the first glance they seemed
    to be
But made of perfume and frivolity.
Handsome they were, but through their comely
    mien
A grinning demon might be clearly seen.
April has flowers where lurk the slugs between.

"Big Joss and little Zeno, pray come here;
Look now—how dreadful! can I help but fear!"
Madame Mahaud was speaker. Moonlight there
Caressingly enhanced her beauty rare,
Making it shine and tremble, as if she
So soft and gentle were of things that be
Of air created and are brought and ta'en
By heavenly flashes. Now, she spoke again:
"Certes, 'tis heavy purchase of a throne
To pass the night here utterly alone.
Had you not slyly come to guard me now,
I should have died of fright outright, I know."
The moonbeams through the open door did fall,
And shine upon the figure next the wall.
Said Zeno, "If I played the marquis part,
I'd send this rubbish to the auction mart;
Out of the heap should come the finest wine
Pleasure and gala-fêtes, were it all mine."
And then with scornful hand he touched the
    thing,
And made the metal like a soul's cry ring.
He laughed; the gauntlet trembled at his stroke.
"Let rest my ancestors!" 'Twas Mahand spoke;
Then murmuring added she, "For you are much
Too small their noble armor here to touch."

And Zeno paled, but Joss with laugh exclaimed,
"Why, all these good black men so grandly
        named
Are only nests for mice. By Jove! although
They lifelike look and terrible, we know
What is within.   Just listen, and you'll hear
The vermins' gnawing teeth; yet 'twould appear
These figures once were proudly named Otho
And Ottocar and Bela and Plato.
Alas! the end's not pleasant—puts one out·
To have been kings and dukes, made mighty rout,
Colossal heroes filling tombs with slain,
And, madame, this to only now remain—
A peaceful nibbling rat to calmly pierce
A prince's noble armor proud and fierce "
"Sing, if you will, but do not speak so loud;
Besides, such things as these," said fair Mahaud,
"In your condition are not understood."
"Well said," made answer Zeno.   " 'Tis a place
Of wonders; I see serpents, and can trace
Vampires, and monsters swarming, that arise
In mist, through chinks, to meet the gazer's
        eyes."
Then Mahand shuddered, and she said, "The
        wine
The abbe made me drink as task of mine
Will soon enwrap me in the soundest sleep;
Swear not to leave me—that you here will keep."
"I swear," cried Joss, and Zeno, "I also;
But now at once to supper let us go."

XIII

THEY SUP

With laugh and song they to the table went.
Said Mahand gayly: "It is my intent
To make Joss chamberlain. Zeno shall be
A constable supreme of high degree."
All three were joyous, and were fair to see.
Joss ate, and Zeno drank; on stools the pair,
With Mahaud musing in the regal chair.
The sound of separate leaf we do not note,
And so their babble seemed to idly float,
And leave no thought behind. Now and again
Joss his guitar made trill with plaintive strain
Or Tyrolean air; and lively tales they told,
Mingled with mirth all free and frank and bold.
Said Mahaud: 'Do you know how fortunate
You are?" "Yes, we are young at any rate;
Lovers half crazy—this is truth at least."
"And more, for you know Latin like a priest
And Joss sings well."
                              "Ah, yes, our master true
Yields us these gifts beyond the measure due."
"Your master! Who is he?" Mahaud ex-
          claimed.
"Satan, we say; but Sin you'd think him
          named,"
Said Zeno, veiling words in raillery.
"Do not laugh thus," she said with dignity;
"Peace, Zeno. Joss, you speak, my chamber-
          lain."

"Madame, Viridis, Countess of Milan,
Was deemed superb; Diana on the mount
Dazzled the shepherd-boy; ever we count
The Isabel of Saxony so fair,
And Cleopatra's beauty all so rare—
Aspasia's, too, that must with theirs compare—
That praise of them no fitting language hath.
Divine was Rhodope; and Venus' wrath
Was such at Erylesis' perfect throat,
She dragged her to the forge where Vulcan
    smote
Her beauty on his anvil.   Well, as much
As star transcends a sequin, and just such
As temple is to rubbish-heap, I say,
You do eclipse their beauty every way.
Those airy sprites that from the azure smile,
Peris and elfs, the while they men beguile,
Have brows less youthful, pure, than yours; be-
    sides,
Disheveled they whose shaded beauty hides
In clouds."
        "Flatt'rer," said Mahaud, "you but sing
Too well."
        Then Joss more homage sought to bring:
"If I were angel under heav'n," said he,
"Or girl or demon, I would seek to be
By you instructed in all art and grace,
And as in school but take a scholar's place.
Highness, you are a fairy bright, whose hand
For scepter vile gave up your proper wand."
Fair Mahand mused, then said, "Be silent
    now;
You seem to watch me; little 'tis I know,

Only that from Bohemia Joss doth come,
And that in Poland Zeno hath his home.
But you amuse me; I am rich, you poor:
What boon shall I confer and make secure?
What gift? Ask of me, poets, what you will,
And I will grant it—promise to fulfill."
"A kiss," said Joss.
    "A kiss!" Quick anger wrought
In Mahand at the minstrel's shameless thought
And flush of indignation warmed her cheek.
"You do forget to whom it is you speak,"
She cried. "Had I not known your high de-
  gree,
Should I have asked this royal boon?" said he.
"Obtained or given, a kiss must ever be.
No gift like king's, no kiss like that of queen!"
"Queen!" And on Mahaud's face a smile was
  seen.

XIV

AFTER SUPPER

But now the potion proved its subtle power,
And Mahaud's heavy eyelids 'gan to lower.
Zeno, with finger on his lip, looked on.
Her head next drooped, and consciousness was
  gone.
Smiling she slept, serene and very fair;
He took her hand, which fell all unaware.

"She sleeps," said Zeno; "now let chance or
  fate
Decide for us which has the marquisate,

And which the girl."
        Upon their faces now
A hungry tiger's look began to show.
"My brother, let us speak like men of sense,"
Said Joss; "while Mahaud dreams in innocence,
We grasp all here, and hold the foolish thing;
Our Friend below to us success will bring.
He keeps his word; 'tis thanks to him I say,
No awkward chance has marred our plans to-
    day.
All has succeeded; now no human power
Can take from us this woman and her dower.
Let us conclude. To wrangle and to fight
For just a yes or no; or to prove right
The Arian doctrines, all the time the Pope
Laughs in his sleeve at you; or with the hope
Some blue-eyed damsel with a tender skin
And milk-white dainty hands by force to win—
This might be well in days when men bore loss
And fought for Latin or Byzantine Cross;
When Jack and Rudolph did like fools contend,
And for a simple wench their valor spend;
When Pepin held a synod at Leptine,
And times than now were much less wise and
    fine.
We do no longer heap up quarrels thus,
But better know how projects to discuss.
Have you the needful dice?"
              "Yes, here they wait
For us."
      "Who wins shall have the marquisate;
Loser, the girl."
        "Agreed."

"A noise I hear?'
"Only the wind that sounds like some one near·
Are you afraid?" said Zeno.
"Naught I fear
Save fasting—and that solid earth should gape.
Let's throw and fate decide, ere time escape."
Then rolled the dice.
"'Tis four."
Twas Joss to throw·
"Six! and I neatly win, you see; and lo!
At bottom of this box I've found Lusace,
And henceforth my orchestra will have place;
To it they'll dance. Taxes I'll raise, and they
In dread of rope and forfeit well will pay·
Brass trumpet-calls shall be my flutes that
    lead;
Where gibbets rise the imposts grow and
    spread."
Said Zeno, "I've the girl, and so is best."
"She's beautiful," said Joss.
"Yes, 'tis confess'd."
"What shall you do with her?" asked Joss.
"I know.
Make her a corpse," said Zeno; "marked you
    how
The jade insulted me just now? Too small
She called me—such the words her lips let fall.
I say, that moment ere the dice I threw
Had yawning Hell cried out, 'My son, for you
The chance is open still: take in a heap
The fair Lusace's seven towns, and reap
The corn and wine and oil of counties ten,
With all their people diligent, and then

Bohemia with its silver mines, and now
The lofty land whence mighty rivers flow
And not a brook returns; add to these counts
The Tyrol with its lovely azure mounts
And France with her historic fleurs-de-lis—
Come now, decide; what 'tis your choice must
    be,'
I should have answered, 'Vengeance give to me
Rather than France, Bohemia, or the fair
Blue Tyrol!   I my choice, O Hell! declare
For government of darkness and of death,
Of grave and worms.'   Brother, this woman
    hath
As marchioness with absurdity set forth
To rule o'er frontier bulwarks of the north.
In any case to us a danger she,
And having stupidly insulted me
'Tis needful that she die.   To blurt all out,
I know that you desire her; without doubt
The flame that rages in my heart warms yours.
To carry out these subtle plans of ours,
We have become as gypsies near this doll—
You as her page, I dotard to control;
Pretended gallants changed to lovers now.
So, brother, this being fact for us to know
Sooner or later, 'gainst our best intent
About her we should quarrel.   Evident
Is it our compact would be broken through.
There is one only thing for us to do,
And that is, kill her.''
                    ''Logic very clear,''
Said musing Joss, ''but what of blood shed
    here?''

Then Zeno stooped and lifted from the ground
An edge of carpet; groped until he found
A ring, which, pulled, an opening did disclose,
With deep abyss beneath; from it there rose
The odor rank of crime. Joss walked to see
While Zeno pointed to it silently.
But eyes met eyes, and Joss, well pleased, was
    fain
By nod of head to make approval plain.

XV
THE OUBLIETTES

If sulphurous light had shone from this vile well
One might have said it was a mouth of hell,
So large the trap that by some sudden blow
A man might backward fall and sink below.
Who looked could see a harrow's threatening
    teeth,
But lost in night was everything beneath.
Partitions, blood-stained, have a reddened
    smear,
And terror unrelieved is master here.
One feels the place has secret histories
Replete with dreadful murderous mysteries,
And that this sepulcher, forgot to-day,
Is home of trailing ghosts that grope their way
Along the walls where specter reptiles crawl.
"Our fathers fashioned for us after all
Some useful things," said Joss; then Zeno
    spoke:
"I know what Corbus hides beneath its cloak;
I and the osprey know its ancient walls,
And how was justice done within its halls."

"And are you sure that Mahand will not wake?"
"Her eyes are closed as now my fist I make;
She is in mystic and unearthly sleep;
The potion still its power o'er her must keep."
"But she will surely wake at break of day?"
"In darkness."
          "What will all the courtiers say
When in the place of her they find two men?"
"To them we will declare ourselves, and then
They at our feet will fall."
              "Where leads this hole?"
"To where the crow makes feast and torrents
      roll—
To desolation.   Let us end it now."

These young and handsome men had seemed to
      grow
Deformed and hideous; so doth foul black heart
Disfigure man, till beauty all depart.
So too the hell within the human face
Transparent is.   They nearer move apace;
And Mahaud soundly sleeps as in a bed.
"To work."
          Joss seizes her and holds her head,
Supporting her beneath her arms, in his;
And then he dared to plant a monstrous kiss
Upon her rosy lips, while Zeno bent
Before the massive chair, and with intent
Her robe disordered as he raised her feet,
Her dainty ankles thus their gaze to meet.
And while the mystic sleep was all profound,
The pit gaped wide, like grave in burial-ground.

XVI

WHAT THEY ATTEMPT BECOMES DIFFICULT

Bearing the sleeping Mahand, they moved now,
Silent and bent, with heavy step and slow.
Zeno faced darkness, Joss turned toward the
    light
So that the hall to Joss was quite in sight.
Sudden he stopped, and Zeno, "What now!"
    called;
But Joss replied not, though he seemed appalled,
And made a sign to Zeno, who with speed
Looked back. Then seemed they changed to
    stone indeed,
For both perceived that in the vaulted hall
One of the grand old knights ranged by the
    wall
Descended from his horse. Like phantom he
Moved, with a horrible tranquillity.
Masked by his helm, toward them he came; his
    tread
Made the floor tremble, and one might have said
A spirit of th' abyss was here. Between
Them and the pit he came—a barrier seen;
Then said, with sword in hand and visor down,
In measured tones that had sepulchral grown
As tolling bell, "Stop, Sigismond, and you,
King Ladislaus;" at those words, though few,
They dropped the marchioness, and in such a
    way
That at their feet like rigid corpse she lay.

The deep voice speaking from the visor's grate
Proceeded, while the two in abject state
Cowered low.   Joss paled, by gloom and dread
     o'ercast,
And Zeno trembled like a yielding mast.
"You two who listen now must recollect
The compact all your fellow-men suspect.
'Tis this: 'I, Satan, god of darkened sphere,
The king of gloom and winds that bring things
     drear,
Alliance make with my two brothers dear,
The Emperor Sigismond and Polish King
Named Ladislaus.   I to surely bring
Aid and protection to them both alway,
And never to absent myself or say
I'm weary.   And yet more: I, being lord
Of sea and land, to Sigismond award
The earth, to Ladislaus all the sea,
With this condition: that they yield to me
When I the forfeit claim, the king his head,
But shall the emperor give his soul instead.' "
Said Joss, "Is't he? Specter with flashing eyes,
And art thou Satan come us to surprise?"
"Much less am I, and yet much more.
O kings of crimes and plots! your day is o'er,
But I your lives will only take to-day;
Beneath the talons black your souls let stay
To wrestle still."
                    The pair looked stupefied
And crushed.   Exchanging looks, 'twas Zeno
     cried,
Speaking to Joss, "Now who—who can it be?"
Joss stammered, "Yes, no refuge can I see;

The doom is on us.   But O specter! say
Who are you?"
              "I'm the judge."
                         "Then mercy, pray."
The voice replied: "God guides His chosen
      hand
To be th' avenger in your path to stand.
Your hour has sounded; nothing now indeed
Can change for you the destiny decreed,
Irrevocable quite.   Yes, I looked on.
Ah, little did you think that any one
To this unwholesome gloom could knowledge
      bring
That Joss a kaiser was, and Zeno king.
You spoke just now, but why?   Too late to
      plead.
The forfeit's due, and hope should all be dead.
Incurables!   For you I am the grave,
O miserable men, whom naught can save!
Yes, Sigismond a kaiser is, and you
A king, O Ladislaus! it is true.
You thought of God but as a wheel to roll
Your chariot on—you who have king's control
O'er Poland and its many towns so strong;
You, Milan's duke, to whom at once belong
The gold and iron crowns; you, emperor made
By Rome, a son of Hercules 'tis said;
And you of Spartibor.   And your two crowns
Are shining lights; and yet your shadow frowns
From every mountain land to trembling sea.
You are at giddy heights twin powers to be
A glory and a force for all that's great;
But 'neath the purple canopy of state

Th' expanding and triumphant arch you prize,
'Neath royal power that sacred veils disguise,
Beneath your crowns of pearls and jeweled
    stars,
Beneath your exploits terrible and wars,
You, Sigismond, have but a monster been,
And, Ladislaus, you are scoundrel seen.
Oh, degradation of the scepter's might
And sword's, when Justice has a hand like
    night,
Foul and polluted! and before this thing,
This hydra, do the temple's hinges swing.
The throne becomes the haunt of all things
    base!
O age of infamy and foul disgrace!
O starry heavens looking on the shame,
No brow but reddens with resentful flame;
And yet the silent people do not stir!
O million arms! what things do you deter;
Poor sheep, whom vermin-majesties devour,
Have you not nails with strong desiring power
To rend these royalties, that you so cower?
But two are taken—such as will amaze
E'en hell itself, when it on them shall gaze.
Ah, Sigismond and Ladislaus, you
Were once triumphant, splendid to the view,
Stifling with your prosperity; but now
The hour of retribution lays you low.
Ah, do the vulture and the crocodile
Shed tears? At such a sight I fain must smile.
It seems to me 'tis very good sometimes
That princes, conquerors stained with bandits'
    crimes,

Sparkling with splendor, wearing crowns of
    gold,
Should know the deadly sweat endured of old—
That of Jehoshaphat; should sob and fear,
And after crime th' unclean be brought to bear.
'Tis well! God rules; and thus it is that I
These masters of the world can make to lie
In ashes at my feet.   And this was he
Who reigned! and this a Cæsar known to be!
In truth, my old heart aches with very shame
To see such cravens with such noble name.
But let us finish: what has just passed here
Demands thick shrouding, and the time is
    near.
Th' accursed dice that rolled at Calvary
You rolled a woman's murder to decree.
It was a dark disastrous game to play,
But not for me a moral to essay.
This moment to the misty grave is due,
And far too vile and little human you
To see your evil ways.   Your fingers lack
The human sense to test your actions black.
What use in darkness mirror to uphold?
What use that now your deeds should be
    retold?
Drink of the darkness, greedy of the ill
To which from habit you're attracted still,
Not recognizing in the draught you take
The stench that your atrocities must make.
I only tell you that this burdened age
Tires of your Highnesses that soil its page,
And of your villainies; and this is why
You now must swell the stream that passes by

Of refuse filth. Oh, horrid scene to show
Of these young men and that young girl just
 now!
Oh, can you really be of human kind
Breathing pure air of heaven? Do we find
That you are men? Oh, no! for when you laid
Foul lips upon the mouth of sleeping maid
You seemed but ghouls that had come furtively
From out the tombs. Only a horrid lie
Your human shape; of some strange, frightful
 beast
You have the soul. To darkness I at least
Remit you now. Oh, murderer Sigismond
And Ladislaus pirate! both beyond
Release—two demons that have broken ban!
Therefore 'tis time their empire over man
And converse with the living, should be o'er.
Tyrants, behold your tomb your eyes before!
Vampires and dogs, your sepulcher is here;
Enter!''
   He pointed to the gulf so near.
All terrified, upon their knees they fell.
''Oh, take us not in your dread realm to dwell!''
Said Sigismond.
   ''But, phantom, do us tell
What thou wouldst have from us; we will obey.
Oh, mercy! 'Tis for mercy now we pray.''
''Behold us at your feet, O specter dread!''
And no old crone in feebler voice could plead
Than Ladislaus did.

   But not a word
Said now the figure motionless, with sword

EVIRADNUS.

—Victor Hugo, Vol. XVII., p. 131.

In hand. This sovereign soul seemed to com-
 mune
With self beneath his metal sheath; yet soon
And suddenly, with tranquil voice said he,
"Princes, your craven spirit wearies me.
No phantom—only man am I. Arise!
I like not to be dreaded otherwise
Than with the fear to which I'm used; know me,
For it is Eviradnus that you see!"

XVII

THE CLUB

As from the mist a noble pine we tell
Grown old upon the heights of Appenzel,
When morning freshness breathes round all the
 wood,
So Eviradnus now before them stood,
Opening his visor, which at once revealed
The snowy beard it had so well concealed.
Then Sigismond was still as dog at gaze,
But Ladislaus leaped, and howl did raise,
And laughed and gnashed his teeth, till, like a
 cloud
That sudden bursts, his rage was all avowed.
" 'Tis but an old man after all!" he cried.

Then the great knight, who looked at both, re-
 plied,
"O kings! an old man of my time can cope
With two much younger ones of yours, I hope.
To mortal combat I defy you both
Singly; or, if you will, I'm nothing loth

With two together to contend.   Choose here
From out the heap what weapon shall appear
Most fit.   As you no cuirass wear, I see,
I will take off my own; for all must be
In order perfect —e'en your punishment.''
Then Eviradnus, true to his intent,
Stripped to his Utrecht jerkin; but the while
He calmly had disarmed, with dexterous guile
Had Ladislaus seized a knife that lay
Upon the damask cloth, and slipped away
His shoes; then barefoot, swiftly, silently,
He crept behind the knight, with arm held high.
But Eviradnus was of all aware,
And turned upon the murderous weapon there,
And twisted it away; then in a trice
His strong colossal hand grasped like a vice
The neck of Ladislaus, who the blade
Now dropped; over his eyes a misty shade
Showed that the royal dwarf was near to death.

"Traitor!" said Eviradnus in his wrath,
"I rather should have hewn your limbs away,
And left you crawling on your stumps, I say;
But now die fast.''

       Ghastly, with starting eyes,
The king without a cry or struggle dies.
One dead; but lo! the other stands bold-faced,
Defiant; for the knight, when he unlaced
His cuirass, had his trusty sword laid down,
And Sigismond now grasps it as his own.
The monster-youth laughed at the silv'ry beard,
And, sword in hand, a murderer glad appeared.

Crossing his arms, he cried, " 'Tis my turn now!"
And the black mounted knights in solemn row
Were judges of the strife.   Before them lay
The sleeping Mahaud, and not far away
The fatal pit, near which the champion knight
With evil emperor must contend for right,
Though weaponless he was.   And yawned the
    pit
Expectant which should be ingulfed in it.

"Now we shall see for whom this ready grave,"
Said Sigismond, "you dog, whom naught can
    save!"
Aware was Eviradnus that if he
Turned for a blade unto the armory,
He would be instant pierced.   What can he do?
The moment is for him supreme. ˙ But, lo!
He glances now at Ladislaus dead,
And with a smile triumphant and yet dread
And air of lion caged to whom is shown
Some loop-hole of escape, he bends him down.
"Ha! ha! no other club than this I need!"
He cried, as seizing in his hands with speed
The dead king's heels, the body lifted high;
Then to the frightened emperor he came nigh,
And made him shake with horror and with fear
The weapon all so ghastly did appear.
The head became the stone to this strange sling,
Of which the body was the potent string;
And while 'twas brandished in a deadly way,
The dislocated arms made monstrous play
With hideous gestures, as now upside down
The bludgeon corpse a giant force had grown.

" 'Tis well!" said Eviradnus, and he cried,
"Arrange between yourselves, you two allied.
If hell-fire were extinguished, surely it
By such a contest might be all relit;
From kindling spark struck out from dead king's
      brow,
Batt'ring to death a living emperor now."

And Sigismond, thus met and horrified,
Recoiled too near the unseen opening wide;
The human club was raised, and struck again—
And Eviradnus did alone remain,
All empty-handed; but he heard the sound
Of specters two falling to depths profound;
Then, stooping o'er the pit, he gazed below,
And, as half-dreaming now, he murmured low,
"Tiger and jackal meet their portion here;
'Tis well together they should disappear!"

XVIII

DAYBREAK

Then lifts he Mahaud to the ducal chair,
And shuts the trap with noiseless, gentle care;
And puts in order everything around,
So that, on waking, naught should her astound.

"No drop of blood the thing has cost," mused he,
"And that is best indeed."
                    But suddenly
Some distant bells clang out.   The mountains
      gray
Have scarlet tips, proclaiming dawning day·

The hamlets are astir, and crowds come out,
Bearing fresh branches of the broom, about
To seek their lady, who herself awakes
Rosy as morn, just when the morning breaks.
Half-dreaming still, she ponders, can it be
Some mystic change has passed, for her to see
One old man in the place of two quite young!
Her wondering eyes search carefully and long.
It may be she regrets the change: meanwhile,
The valiant knight salutes her with a smile,
And then approaching her with friendly mien,
Says, "Madame, has your sleep all pleasant
    been?"

—— ——

THE INFANTA'S ROSE

So small she is! 'Neath a duenna's care,
She looks around with but a listless air,
While holding in her hand a fragrant rose;
What she is gazing at she scarcely knows.
Before her lies a sheet of water; pine
And birch in dark reflection on it shine;
A white-winged swan makes cradle of its waves,
That sway to song of branches which it laves,
And the great garden's radiant flowery show.
She seems an angel molded out of snow.
A stately palace dominates the scene,
With park and fish ponds, where the deer oft
    lean
To drink the waters clear; starred peacocks too
Beneath the ample foliage are in view.

Around this child the grass bears jewels fine—
Rubies and diamonds seem thereon to shine,
While sapphire water flows from dolphins near.
Her innocence takes added whiteness here,
And clust'ring graces trembling aspect wear.

Beside the water, gazing at her flower,
Which quite delights her for the passing hour,
She stands, a figure full of childish grace:
Her bodice is of Genoese point lace,
Her satin skirt has arabesque design,
Worked in gold thread by fingers Florentine.
From urn-like calyx spreads the full-blown rose,
And fills the little hand that holds it close;
Then part the carmine lips as with a smile,
Nostrils dilate, yet with a frown the while
Deep breathing she inhales its fragrance full.
The damask rose, royally beautiful,
So nearly hides her blooming face that we
Scarcely discover where the cheeks may be.
Her sweet blue eyes shine brighter 'neath the
        lines
Of her brown eyebrows; everything combines
To make her incarnation of delight.
What softness in those azure eyes so bright,
What charm in Marie—her dear name that falls
Upon the ear with sound that prayer recalls!
The splendor dazzles, yet we say, "Poor thing!"
Beneath the sky, with all that life may bring
Before her, vaguely great herself she feels;
For her comes spring, and light or shadow steals
Upon the scene; for her the sunsets fine,
And gorgeous luster of the starlight shine;

For her brooks murmur, though themselves un-
   seen;
And Nature's fields, eternal and serene,
She views with gravity that queens must show.
No man she'd seen who did not humbly bow;
Duchess of Brabant she would one day be,
And govern Flanders, or by southern sea
Sardinia, for the young Infanta she,
Five years of age, disdaining common things,
For thus it happens to the babes of kings.
Their white brows something like a shadow bear,
And with their tottering step begins the air
Of royalty.   Rejoicing in her flower,
She waits the gathering empire for her dower.
Her royal look already says " 'Tis mine,"
While with the love she wins vague awe doth
   twine.
Should sudden danger looker-on appall,
The scaffold's shadow on his brow would fall
Who' her, unbidden, snatched from peril dread.

The sweet child smiled, as though in thought
   she said,
"It is enough to live 'mong flowers I love,
With this my rose in hand and heaven above."

Day fades, the wrangling twitter of the nests,
With purple shadow on the trees, attests
The sunset; while each marble goddess' brow
Flushes at eve with ruddy lifelike glow,
As she the mystery of night must show.
All things grow calm; the sun the wave receives
As birds are hidden by the sheltering leaves.

While smiles the child, contented with her flower,
In the vast palace dwells a dreadful power,
Papistical.   The lancet windows shine
Like miters.   Through the glass a dim outline
Is seen of figure pacing to and fro;
From room to room its shadow seems to go,
Or else immovable the long hours through
With brow against the glass, and motionless
As monumental stone, yet not the less
The phantom is a horror, wan and dread,
Its step as slow as bell that tolls the dead.
And death it is—unless it be the king,
With lengthened shadow that the night hours
      bring.
'Tis he—the man a trembling nation fears—
Who thus a phantom horrible appears;
Upright, with shoulder 'gainst the chamber wall,
On whom the twilight can but dimly fall,
This frightful being, in the shadow seen,
Sees nothing of the lovely garden sheen,
Or thickets where the pecking birds have been,
Or child, or shining rippled waters spread,
Reflecting back the evening sky o'erhead.
Oh, no; those glassy orbs, 'neath cruel brows,
Like ocean depths no plummet ever knows,
See mirage that the senses seems to blind.
Could we but know the image in his mind
'Twould be a fleet of noble Spanish ships
That doth all former armaments eclipse.
He sees the vessels fly before the breeze,
Breasting the crested foaming waves with ease;
The rattling of the bellowing sails he hears,
And sees the isle his great Armada nears—

Beneath the stars, a white rock clothed in mist
Which o'er the waves doth to his thunders list.

This is the vision which now fills the soul
Of him who would humanity control,
And blinds him to all else. The floating host
He looks upon as lever he may boast
Shall raise the world; he follows it in thought
Across the darkness of the sea. Thus wrought
In spirit he a conqueror feels, and so
His mournfulness a gleam of light doth know.

The Koran's Iblis and the Bible's Cain
Hardly had stigmas that as black remain
As that which rests on Second Philip's fame;
A being terrible he was, whose name
Meant evil with the ready sword in hand—
A nightmare that o'ershadowed every land.
This royal specter of the Escurial,
Son of the specter called Imperial,
Inspired such terror that a lurid light
Seemed from his presence only to affright.
Men trembled if they merely saw pass by
One of his stewards, for his power seemed
      nigh
To that of the Almighty, so confused
Were they by his determined will, so used
To think of him as changeless and as stable
As are the stars and heaven's abyss, and able
All things to compass; for they thought his will
Cramped destiny, its purpose to fulfill.
The Indies and America he swayed,
Pressed upon Africa, and made afraid

All Europe; yet did gloomy England still
His mind with feelings of disquiet fill.
His mouth was closed, his soul a mystery,
His throne a fraud, based on chicanery.
He was sustained by darkness, as might be
His figure on a dark horse, did we see
Equestrian statue of him; black his wear,
Giving to this so potent prince the air
Of mourning his existence silently;
And like consuming, silent sphinx was he.
Being all-potent, what had he to say?
No one had ever seen him smiling gay;
On iron lips like his smiles could not dwell—
Lips only lighted like the gates of hell.
When he shakes off his torpid adder state,
'Tis to assist tormentors, and to sate
His hateful passion for the death-pyre's air,
Till in his eyeball rests its horrid glare.
With all humanity he is at strife,
With thought and freedom and progressive life;
A slave to Papal Rome, his was the shame
To rule as Satan in Christ's holy name.
The thoughts that flowed from his nocturnal
    mind
Were stealthy, gliding broods of viper kind.
Th' Escurial, Burgos, Aranjuez, his homes,
Never beneath their frigid palace domes
Knew festal scenes where merriment inthralls;
Auto-da-fés made courtly festivals,
And treachery was pastime. Troubled kings
Have often in dim vision night-time brings
Their projects opened, and his dreams had power
A weight of evil on the world to shower.

.They prompted conquest and oppression vast;
Lightnings came from them to destroy and blast;
Even the people that he thought of said,
"We stifle!" such the abject terror dread,
Throughout his empire, of his glance and scowl.
Charles was the vulture, Philip is the owl.

Mournful he looked in pourpoint black for coat,
The Golden Fleece suspended from his throat;
The frigid sentinel of destiny
He seemed—with figure motionless, and eye
Resembling vent hole of a cavern dark;
With finger stretched his will to dimly mark,
Though none there be the gesture who can see.
He holds command by immobility,
And vaguely writes behest to shadows, while—
Oh, strange, unheard-of thing!—a smile
Grinds on his lips, sardonic, bitter, stern,
Born of the vision which he can discern.
Ever more plainly now he gloats to see
His armament in all its majesty.
In thought he views it following his designs,
As if he from the zenith ruled its lines;
And all goes well: calm rolls the ocean dark
As if th' Armada awed it, as the Ark
Of old the Deluge.   He beholds his fleet
Spread out in sailing order, all complete,
The vessels guarding certain spaces fixed
Like chessmen on a chessboard deftly mixed.
The decks and masts and bridges undulate
Like one vast hurdle; waves are subjugate,
And form a hedge around this sacred force;
The currents' work it is to make their course

An aid to debarkation; rocks change mien
And round the ships the circling waves are seen
As if all love; the surf in pearl-drops falls,
And all the galleys have their prodigals
Of strength: see those of Escaut and Adour,
And hundred colonels that the vessels bore
With constables; and Germany has lent
Her ships redoubtable; and Naples sent
Her brigs; and Cadiz, galleons; Lisbon, men
For they were lions that were needed then.
Philip, o'erleaping space, leans o'er the scene,
And hears as well as sees.   With gloating mien
He hears the drums and speaking - trumpets
    shout,
And signal-cries, and hurrying about;
He hears the boatswain's whistle, and the rush
Of agile youths and sailors in the crush
Of hammock hauling; black sepulchral show
Of hubbub on his senses now does grow.
Are they great cormorants or citadels?
The sails make dull, harsh noise, as each one
    swells
Like beating of great wings; and groans the sea
Beneath the mighty mass that noisily
Expands itself and swiftly rolls along.
The somber king smiles at the mighty throng,
Gloating like hungry vampire o'er his prey.
Four hundred vessels! and he knows that they
Bear eighty thousand swords.   O England,
    pale,
He holds thee fast!   What now can aught avail?
The match is near the powder.   'Tis his right
The thunderbolt to hold.   Who has the might

To loose the sheaf from out his potent hand,
Whose orders none can dare to countermand;
Is he not heir to Cæsar—he to-day
Whose shadow spreads from Ganges far away
Even to Posilipo's famous hill?
Is not all ended when he says "I will"?
Is it not he who holds fast Victory still
By the hair?   What can his purposes withstand?
Was it not Philip, he alone who plann'd
This terrifying fleet to pilot now
Its onward course?   The waves obedient flow;
Did he his little finger but incline
All the winged dragons would obey the sign.
Is he not king, the dismal man whom they,
This monstrous whirlwind swarm, must all obey?

When Beit-Cifresil—so history tells,
Son of Abdallah-Beit—sank the great wells
Of Cairo's mosque, he 'graved above the sod,
"The earth is mine, 'tis heaven belongs to God."
And as all tyrants are the same at heart,
Though things may be confused and seem apart,
What said the sultan then this king doth think.

Meanwhile, upon the basin's silent brink,
Her rose the young Infanta gravely holds,
And, blue-eyed angel, kisses oft its folds.
Quite suddenly a blustering breath of air
The shuddering eve casts o'er the plains so fair.
A boisterous ground-wind ruffles every lake,
And bids the rushes tremble, and doth make
The asphodels and distant myrtle-trees
To shudder; reaching the calm child from these

With sudden blast, it shakes a tree that's near,
While shattering the flower she held so dear,
Leaving alone a thorn.   She stooped to gaze,
And saw upon the stream, with great amaze,
The total ruin of her cherished flower.
She could not comprehend this dreadful power
That dared offend her; and she felt afraid,
As looking up to heaven all dismayed.
The lake so calm just now is full of rage,
And the black foaming waves seem war to wage
With the poor rose-leaves on the water strewed,
Drowning and wrecked by turbulence renewed.
The hundred leaves a thousand waves still meet,
And one can dream upon this watery sheet
We see the ruin of a mighty fleet.
Whereon the staid duenna gravely said
Unto the musing, frightened little maid,
Amazed and puzzled, "Madame, bear in mind
That princes govern all things—save the wind."

LITTLE PAUL

Giving her baby birth, the mother died.
O somber Fate, why thus on sorrow's side?
Why take the mother, and leave the tender child
To one the cold world, also a "mother" styled?

For the young father needs must marry again.
        Ah me!
'Tis soon, at *one*, a pariah to be:

This pretty babe did wrong to have been born!
A good old man then took the thing forlorn—
Its grandsire. Sometimes what scarce is, hath
    care
Of what will be: so now aged arms upbear
In mother-wise an infant—strange but true!
What the poor dead have left, to life to woo;
The old are good for only that; they can
But play the part of good Samaritan
Lend to the weak and fallen loving aid,
And chafe the tiny hands outstretched through
    the cold shade.
Needs some one here must answer pity's cry;
Needs some one here be good beneath black sky,
Lest pity and hope no longer sad hearts bless;
Needs must one lead to baby motherless
The wild-eyed goat, fain verdant hills to rove;
Needs must one here lead little hearts to love;
And, old and weary, with compassion rife,
Foster frail blossoms of the spring of life!
Therefore it was that God, who took the dead,
Thus placed the grandsire in the mother's stead;
And, judging winter best love's warmth to im-
    part,
In an old man made throb a woman's heart.

So little Paul was born, an orphan child
With large blue eyes through which a seraph
    smiled,
Lips blithe with babble as of cherubim,
Small rosy hands that stroked each rosy limb—
Yea, all the angel ere the little man!
And the old sire, by long years pale and wan,

Smiled on him as on heaven where day's just
    born.
Oh, how that even did adore that morn!

He took the child straightway unto his home,
'Mong fields spanned by so vast a skyey dome;
But a little child could fill it. Green the plain,
All odorous with perfume sun and rain
Beguile from woods and waters; while around
Their cot a garden laughed, whose every sound
And sight—birds, flowers, yea, all within those
    bowers—
Caressed the child: unenvious are the flowers.

Within this garden peach and apple grew,
Down-showering blossom on one scrambling
    through;
'Neath willows, waters tremulously gleamed,
With here and there a sudden flash that seemed
White shoulders bare of a nymph; and every
    nest
Murmured the hymn obscure of those love-blest.
All voices that one heard were calm and sweet
Like brooklets 'mong warm mosses at your feet;
While in all subtle sound and silence there
The happy trees a leafy burden bear.
God's paradise, the angels' light and song,
Earth's humbler blissful warbling doth prolong
In summer when no star outshines a flower;
And Paul, an angel made this garden-bower
An Eden, while the soul of all was love.
Oh, in how warm a nest was fledged this hap-
    less dove!

Surely, a garden's a sweet thing! Place there
A baby; add an old man; such the care
God takes to make it perfect. Deeming right
To add to joy of sense the soul's delight,
This Poet with a child perfumes the roses,
Then with an old man the sweet triplet closes.
Among the flowers blooms baby for his part,
While grandsire fosters both with dew of his old
    heart.
Oh, what is sweeter in the month of May,
Oh, what were meeter, Virgil, for thy lay,
Than a babe's naked limbs 'mong daisied
    grass!
'Tis so divine that it is frail, alas!

And Paul at first is weakly. Scarce we know
If he will live; or if again will blow
The bitter blast that wailed o'er mother dying,
Come now to bear her sweet to where she's
    lying.
Paul must be fed; a goat consents with glee:
Soon foster-brother to a kid is he!
Since the kid leaps, the boy to walk is fain,
While anxious grandsire murmurs, "Yes, 'tis
    plain·
Walk must we." Oh, the tiny tottering feet,
Charybdis here, dread Scylla there they meet!
With trembling limbs, knees bent, aye children
    strive,
The happiest and most hapless things alive.
When spring bids blossom, trembles most the
    tree!
One's a proud age; one step's a victory—

And Paul's first step leads on to many another.
Can ye not see, bright eyes of many a mother,
The boy by grandsire followed? Charming
    sight!
"Be careful not to fall. Now, now! That's
    right!"
Paul's brave; he looks, longs, laughs, then sud-
    denly
Starts forward, and the old man, proud as he,
Spreads trembling hands round baby unafraid,
And, himself tottering, lends his tottering aid,
Till the goal's won with peals of merriment.
Oh, try to paint a star, or represent
A forest bathed in golden morning light,
But seek not to describe a child's laugh of de-
    light!
'Tis sacred love, blithe innocence a-flower,
Of grace ineffable the richest dower,
Most glorious bloom of purity—ay, even
Of blossoms fragrant with the breath of heaven;
A smile of bliss that proves God's smile of love!

The grandsire, like the saints of yore who
    strove
On mountain solitudes with God in prayer,
Was just a good bewitched old grandfather.
Against the spell that guilelessly beguiled,
Powerless, he sought sweet council of th' adorèd
    child;
He watched the dawn that shone the clear eyes
    through,
While every month Paul babbled something
    new—

Through bonds of speech thought's fitful flut-
    terings,
That hesitate a while on half-plumed wings,
Rise but to fall, then float more blithe and
    strong,
And failing earthly words, alight on heavenly
    song!
Paul captured sounds to set them quickly free,
Some strophe scanned of wondrous melody,
Chattered, lisped, laughed, was never an in-
    stant still,
And the whole house with rapture did full fill.
With laughter and song he made perpetual May;
His waking word was sign of holiday;
All the trees talked of this delightful elf.
Poor little Paul was happiness itself!

By might of smiles which still are deaf to
    "Nay,"
Paul reigned; his grandsire being his docile
    prey,
Happy in strict obedience. "Wait for me,
Father!" He waited. "Come!" Straightway
    came he.
Spring's right to bind old winter with a chain.
What a blithe little household made these twain!
This despot-child an old man loves to obey,
Like January fain to pleasure May.
How, 'mid the song of birds, rich flower-scents
Wandered delightedly these innocents—
One two, gold-haired; and one fourscore and
    gray:
One oft forgetful, one remembering aye—

The child.   Night had no power to make them
    grieve.
Grandsire taught Paul to think who taught
    him to believe.
You had said, beholding morn thus dwell with
    even,
That each showed each sweet diverse sides of
    heaven.

They mingled all—their games by day, by night
Their dreams: what love-bonds did these twain
    unite!
But one bower had they, and were never parted;
Like the first steps, so the first words they
    started,
While hour by hour their pure hearts closelier
    beat.
The grandsire knew no accent soft and sweet
Enough to teach his angel-scholar spell,
And murmur: "Little Paul, oh, loved too well!"
Exquisite dialogues! notes ineffable,
Such as in fairy-tales the bluebirds trill!
"Don't go too near the water.   Ah, now look!
Paul, you have wet your feet."   "It was the
    brook."
"Those stones are slippery."   "Yes, papa."
    "Now run!"
And heaven laughed blue above, and bright the
    sun
Shone, as triumphant and resplendent now,
To see an old man kiss a child's pure brow.

Meantime Paul's father with his new wife dwelt.
No more the presence of the dead is felt

When in her place there smiles another one.
And by this second wife he had a son;
But Paul knew nothing. What if he had? No
    fear
Could reach him, hand in hand with his own
    dear
Kind grandpapa!
                But the grandfather died.

When Sem to Rachel, to Ruth old Boaz cried,
"Weep; I depart!" the women, kneeling near,
Sobbed; but the children cannot—never a tear
Bedims the blithe blue eyes. When with a sigh
The old man said: "Paul, little Paul, I die!
No longer wilt thou see poor grandpapa
Who loves thee!" Naught such mournful words
    could mar
The child's bright innocent life of song, love,
    bliss;
Still gayly he laughed.

                A rustic church there is,
Poor as the lowly roofs that nestle nigh.
It opened: in the funeral train was I.
The humble priest, vague prayers low mur-
    muring,
With friends and kindred from his home doth
    bring
That gentle sire, to lay him low in earth;
And round that sorrow shone the field's May-
    mirth—
For flowers can smile on those in black arrayed!
Mingling hushed voices, good old gossips
    prayed.

We wound along a deep and narrow way:
On either side green fields where cattle lay
Regarding us with large eyes mild and sad;
In summer smocks the peasants all were clad;
And little Paul followed the humble bier.
To the graveyard his kind old friend we bear.
'Tis a lone spot low crumbling walls inclose,
Where only simple folk seek last repose.
No lofty tombs, false epitaphs, are there,
But grassy mounds with crosses black and bare;
Drear spot, yet shielding some from sorrow and
     sin.
By night a wooden wicket shuts it in,
To the bars of which dense ivy-tangles cling.
The little child (a strange remembered thing!)
Was seen to gaze intently at this gate.

To children but as fancy is stern fate,
While to their wondering eyes life's but a dream.
Alas! night darkens round the starry beam.
But three years old was Paul.

                         "You wretched child!
Young Satan! Imp! Be off! You drive me
     wild.
I'll beat him black and blue! Too good am I
To let the little brat come ever nigh.
He's stained my gown! He's spilt the milk!
     For that,
Dry bread, the cellar! And what an ugly brat!"
To whom these words? To Paul. Poor gentle
     heart!
Scarce had he watched dear grandpapa depart,

Than one came to th' old home with loveless
    air—
His father; a woman next with bosom bare,
Suckling a child—his happy little brother.

At once the woman loathed him. Than a
    mother
What sphinx more strange? Whose heart so
    wondrous, say?
On this side darkness, and on that side day!
To her own child honey, to another's stone!
To bear when suffering's sacredness is known
Is well; but a child, gay sprite with golden hair,
Cruel it is such suffering *he* should bear!
The thorn that stabs, for the oak that screened
    of late
What bitter change! In love's sweet stead fell
    hate!

Paul understood it not. When he stole back
At dusk, his little room seemed strangely black.
Long hours he wept, yet scarce knew why,
    indeed,
But felt the vague, chill fear o' the shuddering
    reed.
Waking, he wondered at so dull a morn.
Ah, why then are these little sufferers born?
The house was windowless to let in day,
And dawn no longer seemed to smile his way.
If he crept nigh, "Be off! I want not you!"
His "mother" cried; and slowly Paul withdrew.
'Twas as a cradle drowning in heaven's sight.
The child who made all joyous, lost delight;

His sorrow saddened even the flowers and birds;
For blithe call-notes a volley of bitter words!
"He's odious, with his slinking dirty ways!"
She took his toys her little one to please.
And all Paul's father allowed—so amorous he!
An angel once, a leper now to be!
Once the wife muttered· "Would the brat were
    dead!"

By a caress that dreadful curse was sped:
The *curse* was Paul's.

         "Come thou, my love, my bliss!
O God, the fairest of thy angels this!
A bit of heaven I've stole to swaddle him:
A child he is, but like the cherubim!
God's paradise is in my arms! Oh, see,
How beautiful! I adore thee! Soon thou'lt be
A little man. Oh, what a weight he is!
As heavy as many a toddling boy! I kiss
Thy tiny feet, my life, my love, my sky!"
And Paul remembered, with the memory
Possessed by rose or lamb or little bird,
Long, long ago the sweet same notes he'd heard.
He took his meals in a dark nook, on the floor,
Seeming quite dumb; at length he sobbed no
    more.
To silent suffering oft a child's soul's braced.

Nigh always sadly at the door he gazed.

The child one evening, looked for everywhere,
Could not be found. 'Twas winter, season drear,

Whose soul of hate by night deals direst blow·
Small footsteps then are quickly lost in snow.

They found the child upon the morrow morn:
For some remembered faint cries past .them
    borne
At nightfall; one had even laughed to hear
Midst the weird wonted sounds that throng the
    air
A voice that seemed "Papa, papa!" to call.
Such tidings the whole village did appall.
All sought: the child was in the churchyard
    lone.
Calm as the night, and pallid as a stone,
Outstretched before the gate, quite cold, he lay.
How he had found this sad spot, who shall say,
Alone, by night, unlit by lamp or star?
One of his little hands clutched tight the bar
He vainly tried to open; feeling there
Was one within who yet for little Paul would
    care,
Long, long he had called and sobbed 'mid dark-
    ness dread,
And then had fallen upon the cold earth, dead.
Quite close to his old, kind grandpapa he'd crept
And, powerless even to awaken *him*, fast slept.

THE VOICE OF A CHILD ONE YEAR OLD

WHAT saith he?   Think you he speaks?   Nay,
    I am sure.
But unto whom?   To some one in the azure—
To that we call a spirit; to space, to the sweet
Shiver of the invisible passing wing,
To the shade, the breeze; to his little brother
    dead.
The child a fragment of his heaven-home bears;
Guileless he comes; man, thou receivest him.
He hath the tremor of young leaves and grass.
Prattle before full speech is as the flower
Ere the fruit blooming, lovelier and holier;
For to be lovelier is to be more holy.
The child, pure-souled, on the threshold of sad
    life,
Regards this earth so strange and formidable,
Knows it not, opes wide eyes, and missing God,
Stammers, all-trustful—touching little voice!
The darling weeping with the darling singing
Ends.   His first words like his first steps have
    fear;
Then blooms sweet hope.

            In heaven whereto our sight
Attains not, floats one knows not what fair mist
Of forms which children, reverenced of yore,
Perceive from earth, and which to them lends
    speech.

This child perchance beholds a bright eye shine,
And questions it; in the clear clouds he sees
Faces resplendent, row o'er wondrous row,
And vital phantoms, which for us were void,
Regard him with divine translucent smiles.
O'er him the dusk serene extends its boughs;
He laughs, for unto a child all glooms are
    bright.
'Tis there, in mystery, 'mid the splendor's depths,
With these sweet spirits unknown he lisps and
    laughs;
The child makes question and the spirit replies.
The baby-babble unto blue heaven floats,
Then returns softly, with the waverings
Of the small bird that marks the halcyon soar.
We call that stammering! 'Tis in sooth the
    abysm
Where, as a wingèd being from height to height
Soars, the speech sweet with Eden and with
    dawn
Striveth to seize from utmost heaven a word,
Seeks it and finds, takes it and leaves, and
    quivers.
Through every child's breath thrills the breath
    of heaven.
When with the deep benignant shadow he chats,
The thrush, enraptured, at the edge o' the nest
Uplifts her, while her fledgelings, pensive, frail,
Push through her downy wings their callow
    heads.
The mother seems to say to them: "Ay, listen,
And try to chirp as beautifully." The spring,
Aurora, the blue paradisal day,

Sun-rays—gold darts bright-piercing the dim
    earth—
Melt in a rhythm obscure 'mid the small song
Of this frail spirit and this trembling heart.
To tremble, totter, prattle, is the charm
Of th' age when through a tear bright laughter
    gleams.
Oh, heavenly shadow and shine of infant-speech!
The child seems forceful to assuage harsh fate.
From the small child sweet lessons nature learns·
This rosy mouth's the tiny gate august
Whence falls—oh, majesty of the frail, bare be-
    ing—
Upon the gulf unknown the unknown Word.
What largess!—innocence made ev'n our guest!
What gift of heaven! Who knows the starry
    lore,
The beams of bounty, who knows the faith, the
    love,
Which through their trembling twilight ever
    shed,
Amid the bitter strife wherein we dwell,
The souls of children on the souls of men?
Sounds one the depth of this soft speech where-
    through
One feels pass all that thrills the innocent?
No. Men deep-stirred hearken these tender
    strifes
Of syllables scattered in the golden dawn—
Speech wherein heaven hath left a starry trace—
But comprehend not, pass it by, and say,
" 'Tis naught; or but a breath, a murmur, sigh;
The word is senseless till the spirit be ripe."

How know you that? This cry, this nest-born
    chant
Is of an angel changing to a man.
Adore it! The melodious sound—the scale
Floating and free, where infancy makes one
The perfume of its lips, its eyes pure blue—
Resembles, wind of heaven, those wondrous
    words
Which, to declare midnight or day, thou lendest
To the vast soul obscure through all things shed.

The being born to the light of this false world
Lisps as he can his sad and sweet surprise.
For the animal in the deep enigma lost,
All comes of man. Into this world man casts
A faint clew to the mystery, and through him
A little day lightens the problem dark.
Ah, yes, this warble, music vague and soft,
Pure mist of words divine, confused like foam,
Song whose sweet secret hold the newly born,
Which from the cottage floateth to the wood,
Is a world-language, an exchange eterne
Of dawn with stars, with th' angel of God man's
    soul :
Nest-idiom, cradle-interpreter, aye sent
By the little children to the little birds.

ARISTOPHANES

UNDER the willows to and fro young virgins
Walk; round bare shoulders cluster golden curls;
The amphora on white brows cannot prevent,
When fair Menalcus comes, a slackening step
And soft word: "Hail, Menalcus!" while the
    leaves,
Awakened by the mocking laughter of birds,
In the amorous encounter take glad part;
Beneath the lovely boughs so many sweets
Are snatched, the amphora reaches home half-
    filled.
The grandam, glancing sharply o'er thread she
    winds,
Grumbles, "What hast thou done, who hath
    caught thy hand,
That all the water on the way is spilt?"
The maiden answers: "I know not," and dreams.
What time the cool hill-shadow in the meads
Lengthens, and comes a far-off sound of wheels,
'Tis sweet to dream of destinies storm-driven,
And to prepare one's soul for future days.
'Tis by the little he covets, less he knows,
A man's most wise.   Let's love! Divine is
    spring;
By the small valley-blooms our souls are stirred,
By bounteous April and warm nests ne'er dull,
Th' inviting moss, the roses' perfume sweet,
And the sweet silence of the wild wood-way.
Fair women, mingling voices, to their homes

Return, but at the door some stay to talk.
Wife, of thy husband speaking ill, take heed!
Thy baby boy regards thee with wide eyes.
Muses, revere we Pan, the ivy-crowned!

MOSCHUS

O NYMPHS, in the forest-fountain bathe ye still.
The woods are dark, but though strange voices
    thrill
    Their depths whence eagles take their tireless
    flight,
The darkness is not of that drear excess
Ne'er stirred by sweet Neæra's loveliness,
    As by love's lovely star the somber night.

Neæra's fair, tender, and pure, and lo!
Starwise through darkling thickets she doth
    glow.
    The humming bees cease valley-blooms to mar,
The warm wind frets no longer languid trees.
What saith the wind? and, ah! what hum the
    bees?
    "Clothed, she's a flower; but naked, she's a
    star!"

The stars of heaven envy thee more bright,
Bathing, O chaste one, with that vague affright
    Which with its boldness beauty blends alway,
'Neath foliage whence the eye of Faunus glows.
Subtle and sweet Neæra, well she knows
    Nymphs, naked, turn to goddesses straight-
    way.

For me—albeit a harder lot is mine—
Yet o'er my head the summer sun doth shine
    Through linkèd boughs of many a leafy tree;
The meadows, I, the woods, the wayward wind—
And ah! Neæra, love I; soul-inclined
    Aye unto Pan's soft pastoral melody.

Albeit within life's shade, where oft we weep,
Far, threatening discords roll from steep to
    steep;
    Albeit across love's heaven keen lightnings
    shoot,
While with their flashes love's soft smiles are
    hidden—
Fearless at whiles, to listen is't forbidden
    Betwixt two thunder-peals an amorous flute?

———

RACAN

If all the things the fond soul dreams
    Into winged little loves might quiver,
My voice, which 'neath the starry beams
    Ever aspireth, sinketh ever;

Which mingles in its hymn most tender
    Astrea, Eros, Gabriel,
Angels and gods, whose diverse splendor
    Aye blends, by sovran love's bright spell,

(Like to leaf-cradled nest-broods holding
    Sweet converse with strange lights afar,
Ever beneath warm plumage folding
    The heavenly tones of star on star),

Beneath yon slumb'rous vault serene
　With little airs to help its flying,
Beneath the stars, above the treen—
　O sweet, in innocent sleep soft-sighing,

Toward thee my song would now be wing-
　　ing,
　To reach thee at rosy break of day—
If all the songs one's soul is singing
　Might lift bird-wings and flee away!

BEAUMARCHAIS

To the woods, to the woods, O lovely peasant
　　girls!
Beside the mills, whose beasts of burden are we.
Your bonnets fling, and make our hearts the
　　haunt
Of your caprices, tender, joyous, shy.
'Tis Sunday. Afar one hears the bagpipe squeak;
The wind delights to fret the docile reeds;
Fête in the fields—the order of day's signed
　　"Joy!"
The happy birds, who pipe on quarter-days,
Shift homes as many times as seems them good.
All trembles: ne'er for naught the wood-ways
　　thrill;
The green forked boughs above the hornèd fawns
Stir stealthily; let's imitate the birds.
Ah, the small robbers, how they glory in sin!
Let's help the kerchief to make bare the neck,

Wandering like Chloe and Daphne both afraid.
Not always innocent may mortals be.
But this hour's ours; in the cistus then let's
    sport,
In moss, i' the grass; this silly scandal achieve—
Love; to that godhead archly offer ourselves.
Since green are meadows, since the sky is blue,
Let's love! The idyll with big words is choked;
Tragedy-wise we will not shout nor strut,
But whisper all that whispers in the soul.

———

ANDRÉ CHÉNIER

O SWEET, the charming scandal of the birds
In trees, in flowers, in meadows, 'mong the
    reeds;
Blithe sun-rays bathing eagles in the blue;
Tempestuous gayety of the nereids bare,
Wide flinging foam, and dancing 'mong the
    waves;
Whitenesses which make sailors muse afar;
All-glorious sports of goddesses impearled,
Choosing for couch the seas as thou the leaves—
All that plays on the horizon, lightens, shines,
Hath no more splendor than thy wondrous song.
Thy hymn adds joy ev'n to the joy of gods.
Superb thou stand'st. Also thou lovest *me*,
And on my knee wilt sit. Psyche perchance
At whiles like thee assumes a haughty air,
Then clings to the neck of the young god, her
    lord.

Can one strive long with love? 'Tis to be born;
To taste in the arms of a belovèd being
What honey of heaven God in His creatures
    hives;
An angel 'tis to be, with man's desire.
O Sweet, refuse me naught. Canst *thou* be
    mean?

NATURE

ALL ye who walk with restless, roving eyes,
Bethink ye, Pan knows always where you are.
Lovers, if you with reason are afraid
Lest the dim path disclose your stealthy feet,
Beware! Within that wood ye are ill concealed!
The trembling forest listens, looks, and longs;
All the dark tangled wood-ways are astir;
Fear lest your kisses agitate the copse,
The strenuous shudder of leafy branches, fear!
Nature is not of marble—'tis a spirit;
That strange sweet breath which flows thro'
    twilight sweet
Ye take for April's softest air, is love.
Like water-drops are ye, the world's the cup;
Lovers, one sigh makes ecstasy o'erflow.
Above your foreheads all the trembling boughs
Mingle their voices, perfumes, incense, songs;
Man's passion floods the forest, dark, profound,
And the wild Dryad whirls with lifted skirt.

TWILIGHT

WITH a vague dreamful hymn the aspen-leaves
    are stirred;
Belated travelers, to walk alone afeared,
Lift voices through the twilight, onward hasten-
    ing:
        O suffer each timid bird
            Sing.

The weary mariners are cradled on the main;
Blue waves, wherewith the noontide mingles hot
    gold rain,
Find ease, for the sun is set, and almost cease
    to weep:
        O suffer all sorrow, all pain
            Sleep!

Ah! though to-day be dark, one dreams a bright
    to-morrow;
Dim tearful eyes toward heaven are raised some
    blue to borrow.
Godward our hope is winged; God speeds it on
    the way:
        O suffer all pain, all sorrow
            Pray!

'Tis for a purer air that here one fails for breath.
All that above would soar must first be laid be-
    neath;
In earth's last silence all must seek heaven's
    harmony:
        O suffer all fain of death
            Die!

SOLOMON

THE king am I fate's somber puissance fills;
    God's temple build I, and earth's cities raze;
Hiram my slave that toils, Charos that kills,
    Upon me, awestruck, gaze.

My tool to build, my sword to smite, are they,
    Ne'er ceasing toil for weariness or pain;
My breath were strong to turn out of its way
    The Libyan hurricane;

Hence God Himself is troubled. Of a fell
    Crime born, sin's somber wisdom wraps my
        throne;
Satan, to judge betwixt high heaven and hell,
    Would choose King Solomon.

The lord of faith am I, the lord of fear—
    Warrior, I rule the body; priest, the soul.
As king I wield the day's bright azure sphere;
    As pontiff, night control.

I am the subtle master of all dreams;
    I guide the hand that writes upon the wall·
Earth's omens are familiar—sighs, sobs, screams
    I read them one and all.

Mighty am I, and like a god morose;
    Mysterious as an Eden sealed alway.
Yet though my power is mightier than the rose
    Is fragrant in mid May,

O'er one thing doth my golden scepter shine
　Vainly, as 'twere a twig bent by a dove—
I cannot from my soul, O nymph divine
　Affright thy song of love!

Subtle the notes of this winged thing that broods
　In my soul's depths, as in a shadowy tree;
And powerless I to chase it, as spring woods
　To hush bird-melody!

THE EMPEROR'S RETURN

Sire, to thy capital thou shalt come back,
　Without the battle's tocsin and wild stir;
Beneath the arch, drawn by eight steeds coal
　　black,
　Dressed like an emperor.

Thro' this same portal, God accompanying,
　Sire, thou shalt come upon the car of state;
Like Charlemagne, a high ensainted king,
　Like Cæsar, wondrous great.

On thy gold scepter, to be vanquish'd never,
　Thy crimson beakèd bird shall shine anon;
Upon thy mantle all thy bees a-shiver
　Shall twinkle in the sun.

Paris shall light up all her high and hundred
　Tow'rs; shall speak out with all her tones
　　sublime;
Bells, clarions, rolling drums shall all be thun-
　　der'd
　In music at a time.

A mighty people, pale, with steps that falter,
  Shall come to thee, by one attraction drawn,
Awestricken as a priest before the altar,
  Glad as a child at dawn—

A people who would lay all laws e'er sung
  Or storied at thy feet; aye floating on,
Intoxicate, from Bonaparte the young
  To old Napoleon.

Then a new army, burning for the advance,
  In exploit terrible, round thy car shall cry
Amain, "Vive l'Empereur!" and "Vive la
      France!"
  And seeing thee pass by,

Chief of the mighty empire, down shall fall
  People and troops; but thou before their view
Shalt not be able to stoop down at all
  With, "I am pleased with you."

An acclamation, tender, lofty, sweet,
  A heart-song high as ecstasy can bear it,
Shall fill, O captain mine! the city's street,
  But thou shalt never hear it.

Stern grenadiers, the veterans we admire,
  Mute thy steed's steps shall kiss; albeit
A sight pathetic, beautiful, yet, sire,
  Your Majesty shall not see it.

While round thy form gigantic, like a friend,
  France and the world awake in shadows deep,
Here in thy Paris ever, world without end,
  Thou shalt lie fast asleep;

Ay, fast asleep with that same sullen slumber,
  Those fadeless dreams, that on his stone chair
    fix
The Barbarossa, sitting out that number
  Of centuries now six.

Thy sword beside thee, and thine eyelids close,
ʼ Thy hand yet moved by Bertrand's kiss—the
    last;
Upon the bed whence sleeper never rose,
  Thou shalt be stretched full fast—

Like to those soldiers marching bolt upright
  So often after thee to field or town,
Who by the wind of battle touch'd one night
  Suddenly laid them down;

Like sleepers, not like those whose race is run
  With grave, proud attitude of armèd men,
But them that voice of dawn, the morning gun,
  Shall never wake again;

Yea, so much like, that seeing thee all ice,
  Like a mute god permitting ādoration,
They who came smiling, love-drunk, in a trice
  Shall raise a lamentation.

Sire, at that moment thou, for kingdom meet,
  Shall have all beating hearts to be thine own.
Nations shall make thy phantom take a seat,
  A universal throne.

Poets, select, upon their knees in dust,
  Shall hail thee far diviner than of old,

And gild thine altar, stain'd by hands unjust,
  With a sublimer gold.

The clouds shall pass away from thy great glory;
  Nothing to trouble it for aye shall come;
It shall expand itself o'er all our story
  Like a vast azure dome.

Yea, thou shalt be to all a presence solemn,
  Both good and great—to France an exile high
And calm; a brass Colossus on thy column
  To every stranger's eye.

But thou, the while the sacred pomp shall lead
  A cortege such as time hath never heard,
So that all eyes shall seem to see indeed
  A vanished world upstirr'd;

The while they hear, hard by the wondrous
    dome
  Where shadows keep the great names that
      men mark
In Paris still, the old guns growling home
  Their master with a bark;

The while thy name without a peer shall soar,
  Illustrious, beautiful to Heav'n, ah! thou
Shalt in the darkness feel for evermore
  The grave-worm on thy brow.

SOUL STRESS

A LOFTY spirit on march his rumors hath, his
    floods,
His shocks, and makes profoundly quake earth's
    multitudes,
Moving the world around him as ever he walks
    right on.
One who is made not bright with joy, for fear is
    wan.
Man like an ever-changing cloud still traveleth;
Not one, how small soe'er, escapes that mighty
    breath;
The humblest, while he speaks, thrill through
    their inmost being.

Thus when the strong north wind from out the
    horizon fleeing,
Hastening on venturous quest athwart the sea
    and land,
Thick rain and lightning twists, even as a girl
    the band
That girds her slender frame with archest smile
    unbinds,
When the vast blast deep-muttering passeth
    shelter finds
No blade of grass in valley's depth from the
    awful might
And fiery speed of the hurricane's formidable
    flight.

"WHENCE CAME THIS BOOK?"

THE wall of ages in my dream appeared
Of living flesh, and granite rocks upreared—
Fixed immobility by sorrows made!
A building which loud sounds of crowds invade—
Black holes, star-lighted by ferocious eyes,
Mutations strange of grouped monstrosities,
Vast statues, giant frescoes, met the view.
At times the gaping wall showed chambers
    through—
Dens, where there sat the happy and the great,
Victors, crime-stained, with praise intoxicate;
Gilt rooms, of jasper and of porphyry;
And the wall shivered as a wind-blown tree.
All ages, crowned with coin or battlement,
Were there; wan sphinxes, o'er the riddle bent.
Each sat as vaguely living, then was lost
To sight in upper darkness, as a host
Together with its captain petrified.
Soon as to scale the realms of night I tried,
The mass swayed to and fro, as 'twere a cloud—
At once it was a wall, and was a crowd.
The marble clutched the scepter and the sword,
And wept the dust, and the red blood was poured.
In human shape fell every shattered stone;
Man, with th' unknown breath that leads him
    on,
Eve, Adam floating, one and yet diverse,
Throbbed on the wall, and life, and universe,

And fate—black thread that does the tomb di-
vide.
Lightning at times made on the wall's wan side
Millions of faces of a sudden flame;
Then showed that Nothing, which the whole we
name—
Kings, gods, law, glory, and the flow and fate,
Through every time and age, of man's estate.
And 'neath my sight stretched out the dismal
tale
Of hunger, ignorance, plagues, wars, and wail;
And superstition, science, history,
Like a black screen, as far as eye can see.
That wall, built of black ruin, bleak and bare,
Reared itself rugged, mournful, shapeless, where
I know not—hid in darkness far away.

There are no mists, as naught in algebra,
Which can resist in numbers, or in skies,
The fixed, calm search of penetrating eyes.
This wall, which to my sight as first I mused,
Seemed shifting as a wave, vague and confused,
Illusive, vap'rous, giddy, full of change;
Yet 'neath my thoughtful gaze the vision strange
Grew clearer and less dim, as by degrees
My pupils scanned the scene with greater ease.

How then shall we describe this book aright—
Drawn from the past, the tomb, the gulf, the
night?
'Tis the tradition which the tempest feeds
Of revolutions, God unchains and speeds.

After the earthquake shock, what still stands
    fixed,
A wreck, but with the future's vague dawn
    mixed:
Man's onward growth, the ruin of old times,
Which darkness fills, and poetry sublimes·
Palatial charnel-house, in ruined state,
Inhabited by death and built by fate,
Wherein, when not by numbing fear possest,
As birds on wing, or passing sunbeams rest,
Life, liberty, and hope, their own may keep
'Tis the immeasurable, tragic heap
Where in its hideous breach do vipers glide,
And dragons, ere they in their caverns hide,
And mists before they back to heaven won.
This book is the dread wreck of Babylon,
The gloomy tower of things, the home concise
Of right, wrong, mourning, tears, and sacrifice;
Once proud, and ruling o'er horizons far
Now having naught but blocks that hideous are,
Scattered in the dark valley, lost and laid:
It is man's epic—harsh, immense, decayed.

LES RAYONS ET LES OMBRES

YE MARINERS WHO SPREAD YOUR SAILS

YE mariners! ye mariners! each sail to the
  breeze unfurled,
In joy or sorrow still pursue your course around
  the world;
And when the stars next sunset shine, ye anx-
  iously will gaze
Upon the shore, a friend or foe, as the windy
  quarter lays.

The envious souls with spiteful tooth the statue's
  base will bite;
The birds will sing, the bending boughs with
  verdure glad the sight;
The ivy root in the stone entwined will cause old
  gates to fall;
The church-bell sound to work or rest the vil-
  lagers will call.

The glorious oaks will still increase in solitude
  profound,
Where the far west in distance lies as·evening
  veils around;

Ye willows, to the earth your arms in mournful
trail will bend,
And back again your mirror'd forms the water's
surface send.

The nests will oscillate beneath the youthful
progeny;
Embraced in furrows of the earth the germing
grain will lie;
Ye lightning-torches, still your streams will cast
into the air,
Which like a troubled spirit's course float wildly
here and there.

The thunder-peals will God proclaim, as doth
the ocean wave;
The violets will nourish still the flower that April
gave;
Upon your ambient tides will be man's sternest
shadow cast;
Your waters ever will roll on when man himself
is past.

All things that are, or being have, or those that
mutely lie,
Have each its course to follow out, or object to
descry,
Contributing its little share to that stupendous
whole,
Where with man's teeming race combined crea-
tion's wonders roll.
The poet, too, will contemplate th' Almighty
Father's love,
Who to our restless minds, with light and dark-
ness from above

Hath given the heavens, that glorious urn of
    tranquil majesty,
Whence in unceasing stores we draw calm and
    serenity.

HOLYROOD PALACE

PALACE and ruin, bless thee evermore!
Grateful we bow thy gloomy tow'rs before;
For the old King of France * hath found
    in thee
That melancholy hospitality
Which in their royal fortune's evil day,
Stuarts and Bourbons to each other pay.

COME WHEN I SLEEP

OH, when I sleep, come near my resting-place,
    As Laura came to bless her poet's heart;
And let thy breath in passing touch my face,
        At once a space
        My lips will part.

And on my brow where too long weighed su-
    preme
    A vision—haply spent now—black as night,
Let thy look as a star arise and beam,
        At once my dream
        Will seem of light.

---

* King Charles X.

Then press my lips, where plays a flame of bliss—
A pure and holy love-light—and forsake
The angel for the woman in a kiss,
　　At once, I wis,
　　My soul will wake!

———

EARLY LOVE REVISITED

I HAVE wished in the grief of my heart to know
　If the vase yet treasured that nectar so
　　clear,
And to see what this beautiful valley could show
　Of all that was once to my soul most dear.
In how short a span doth all Nature change!
　How quickly she smoothes with her hand
　　serene—
And how rarely she snaps, in her ceaseless range,
　The links that bound our hearts to the scene!

Our beautiful bowers are all laid waste;
　The fir is felled that our names once bore;
Our rows of roses by urchins' haste
　Are destroyed, where they leap the barrier
　　o'er.
The fount is walled in where, at noonday pride,
　She so gayly drank, from the wood descend-
　　ing,
In her fairy hand was transformed the tide,
　And it turned to pearls through her fingers
　　wending.

The wild, rugged path is paved with spars,
  Where erst in the sand her footsteps were
    traced,
When so small were the prints that the surface
    mars .
  That they seemed to smile ere by mine effaced.
The bank on the side of the road, day by day,
  Where of old she awaited my loved approach
Is now become the traveler's way
  To avoid the track of the thundering coach.

Here the forest contracts, there the mead ex-
    tends;
  Of all that was ours, there is little left—
Like the ashes that wildly are whisked by winds;
  Of all souvenirs is the place bereft.
Do we live no more?   Is our hour then gone?
  Will it give back naught to our hungry cry?
The breeze answers my call with a mocking tone,
  The house that was mine makes no reply.

True! others shall pass, as we have passed;
  As we have come, so others shall meet;
And the dream that our mind had sketched in
    haste
  Shall oth_ continue, but never complete.
For none upon earth can achieve his scheme;
  The best as the worst are futile here:
We awake at the self-same point of the dream—
  All is here begun, and finished elsewhere.

Yes! others shall come in the bloom of the heart,
  To enjoy in this pure and happy retreat
All that Nature to timid love can impart
  Of solemn repose and communion sweet.

In our fields, in our paths, shall strangers stray;
In thy wood, my dearest, new lovers go lost;
And other fair forms in the stream shall play
Which of old thy delicate feet have crost.

THE EIGHTEENTH CENTURY

O EIGHTEENTH CENTURY! by Heaven chas-
tised.
Godless thou livedst; by God thy doom was fixed.
Thou in one ruin sword and scepter mixed,
Then outraged love, and pity's claim despised.
Thy life a banquet, but its board a scaffold at
the close,
Where far from Christ's beatic reign Satanic
deeds arose!
Thy writers, like thyself, by good men scorned;
Yet, from thy crimes, renown has decked thy
name,
As the smoke emplumes the furnace flame:
A revolution's deeds have thine adorned!

GASTIBELZA

GASTIBELZA, the man with the carabine,
Sung in this wise:
"Hath one of you here known Donna Sabine
With the gentle eyes?

Ay, dance and sing, for the night draws nigh
  O'er hill and lea.
The wind that wails o'er yon mountain high
Will madden me!

"Hath one of you here known Donna Sabine,
  To me so dear?
Her mother, the old, old Maugrabine,
  Erst made one fear;
For each night from the haunted cavern she'd
    cry
  With an owlet's glee.
The wind that wails o'er yon mountain high
Will madden me!

"Ay, dance ye and sing!   The hour's delight
  One needs must use.
How young she was, and those eyes how
    bright,
  Which made one muse.
To this old man whom a child leads by,
  A coin cast ye!
The wind that wails o'er yon mountain high
Will madden me!

"In sooth the queen for envy had wept.
  Had she seen her, alack!
As o'er Toledo's bridge she light-tript
  In a corset black.
A chaplet of beads that charmed one's eye,
  From her neck hung free.
The wind that wails o'er yon mountain high
Will madden me!

"The king, bedazed with her loveliness,
    Bespake one there:
'For one only smile, for one only kiss,
    One tress of her hair,
I would give my Spain and gold realms that lie
    O'er yonder sea!'
The wind that wails o'er yon mountain high
    Will madden me!

"I know not well if I loved this sweet;
    But well I know
If but one glance of her soul might greet
    My soul, I would go
On the galleys to toil, on the galleys to die,
    Right cheerfully.
The wind that wails o'er yon mountain high
    Will madden me!

"One summer morn when all heaven was bright,
    All earth was gay,
To the stream with her sister for dear delight,
    This sweet must stray.
The foot of her comrade I there did spy,
    And saw *her* knee.
The wind that wails o'er yon mountain high
    Will madden me!

"When thus of me, a poor shepherd, was seen
    This glorious May,
Methought, 'tis Cleopatra the queen
    Who once, they say
Won Cæsar, great emperor of Germany,
    Her slave to be.
The wind that wails o'er yon mountain high
    Will madden me!

"Dance ye and sing!   Lo, the night doth fall!
    Sabine, one while
Her dove like beauty, her soul, her all,
    Her angel-smile,
For a ring of gold to the Count hath sold:
    Saldane is he.
The wind that wails o'er yon mountain high
Will madden me!

"On this bench for a moment suffer me rest—
    Full weary each limb.
With this Count then fled this loveliest—
    Alas, with him!
By the road that leads—   But I know not, I,
    Where then fled she.
The wind that wails o'er yon mountain high
Will madden me!

"I saw her pass at the death of day,
    And all was night.
And now I wander and weary alway,
    In pain's despite.
My soul's on quest; my dagger's put by,
    Ne'er used to be.
The wind that wails o'er yon mountain high
Has maddened me!"

ON A FLEMISH WINDOW PANE

WITHIN thy cities of the olden time
Dearly I love to list the ringing chime,
Thou faithful guardian of domestic worth,
Noble old Flanders! where the rigid north
A flush of rich meridian glow doth feel,
Caught from reflected suns of bright Castile.
The chime, the clinking chime! To Fancy's
    eye—
Prompt her affections to personify—
It is the fresh and frolic hour, arrayed
In guise of Andalusian dancing maid,
Appealing by a crevice fine and rare,
As of a door oped in ''th' incorporal air.''
She comes, o'er drowsy roofs, inert and dull,
Shaking her lap, of silv'ry music full,
Rousing without remorse the drones a-bed,
Tripping like joyous bird with tiniest tread,
Quiv'ring like dart that trembles in the targe,
By a frail crystal stair, whose viewless marge
Bears her slight footfall, tim'rous half, yet free.
In innocent extravagance of glee
The graceful elf alights from out the spheres,
While the quick spirit—thing of eyes and ears
As now she goes, now comes, mounts, and anon
Descends, those delicate degrees upon,
Hears her melodious spirit from step to step run
    on.

THE HUMBLE HOME

THE church* is vast: its towering pride, its
    steeples loom on high;
The bristling stones with leaf and flower are
    sculptured wondrously;
The portal glows resplendent with its "rose,"
And 'neath the vault immense at evening
    swarm
Figures of angel, saint, or demon's form,
    As oft a fearful world our dreams disclose.

But not the huge cathedral's height, nor yet its
    vault sublime,
Nor porch, nor glass, nor streaks of light, nor
    shadows deep with time,
    Nor massy towers, that fascinate mine eyes;
No, 'tis that spot—the mind's tranquillity—
Chamber wherefrom the song mounts cheerily,
    Placed like a joyful nest wellnigh the skies.

Yea! glorious is the church, I ween, but Meek-
    ness dwelleth here.
Less do I love the lofty oak than mossy nest it
    bear;
    More dear is meadow breath than stormy wind
And when my mind for meditation's meant,
The seaweed is preferred to the shore's extent
    The swallow to the main it leaves behind.

---

* The Cathedral Notre Dame of Paris; compare Book
III. chap. i. of the author's romance, "Notre Dame."

GASTIBELZA
—Victor Hugo, Vol XVII., p. 179.

WHEN NOISY RABBLE

WHEN, noisy rabble, you together meet
To track, till you discover, his retreat,
All rousing one another, furious, mad,
"Do you not scent him?" Sober folk and sad
Your cries made dream some dragon in his lair,
With flaming eyes, and scales instead of hair,
Wonder to find the object of your rage
This thoughtful, gentle, kind, mysterious sage.

SWEET MEMORY OF LOVE

As life wanes on, the passions slow depart—
  One with his grinning mask, one with his steel;
Like to a strolling troupe of Thespian art,
  Whose pace decreases, winding past the hill.
But naught can Love's all-charming power
    efface
  That light, our misty tracks suspended o'er.
In joy thou'rt ours; more dear thy tearful grace.
  The young may curse thee, but the old adore.

But when the weight of years bows down the
    head,
  And man feels all his energies decline,
His projects gone, himself tomb'd with the dead,
  Where virtues lie, nor more illusions shine,

When all our lofty thoughts dispersed and o'er,
 We count within our hearts so near congealed
Each grief that's past, each dream—exhausted
    ore!—
 As counting dead upon the battle-field,

As one who walks by the lamp's flickering blaze,
 Far from the hum of men, the joys of earth—
Our mind arrives at last by tortuous ways
 At that drear gulf where but despair has birth.
E'en there, amid the darkness of that night,
 When all seems closing round in empty air,
Is seen through thickening gloom one trembling
    light—
 'Tis Love's sweet memory that lingers there!

———

GUITAR SONG

"How, how, how," asked he,
  "O'er the water-way
Flee false siren's lay?"
  "Row, row, row!" laughed she.

"How, how, how," asked he,
  "Lull for ever and aye
Sorrow and drear dismay?"
  "Sleep, sleep, sleep!" said she.

"How, how, how," asked he,
  "Make one lovely May
Mine for ever and aye?"
  "Love, love, love!" sighed she.

BABY'S SEASIDE GRAVE

BROWN ivy old, grass freshly green, bright
flowers,
Fane where the soul sees One it elsewhere
dreams;
Gay insects murmuring music warm long hours
To the tired shepherd drowsed with summer's
beams;

Winds, waves, aye blending wild sweet har-
mony;
Woods wherein brightest noontide pales to
even;
Ye fruits that gleam from out the dusk-leaved
tree;
Ye stars that gleam from out mysterious
heaven;

Birds with quick joyous cries, billows soft-sigh-
ing;
Cold lizard of the hottest nook still fain;
Fields unto ocean's bounteous love replying—
One giving silvery pearl, one golden grain;

Nature, that wak'st to life, that lull'st to death;
Leaf-cradled nests round which the air scarce
creeps;
Above this mossy cradle hold your breath;—
Leave the child sleeping while its mother
weeps!

A. L.

EACH hope, dear child, is a slender reed.
God holds in His hand frail threads of our
days,
And divides them at pleasure, and takes no heed
That, the thread being cut, our joy falls from
its place:
In each cradle on earth
A death hath birth.

Erewhile, seest thou, the future, pure light,
Shone sweetly before my young spirit a-fire—
Bright bird on the wave, in heaven star bright,
Splendid bloom 'mid the shadow a-throb with
desire:
This vision, my sweet,
How lovely! how fleet!

If, haply, nigh thee one dreamfully weep,
Let the tears fall, nor do thou ask why.
Sweet 'tis to weep—ay, the bright drops keep
Soft melody 'midst the tempestuous world-cry:
O child, every tear
Leaves some sin clear!

TO MADEMOISELLE FANNY DE P.

O THOU whom thy sweet age defends,
  Laugh lightly; all things yet caress.
Play! Sing! Be a child whose joy ne'er ends:
  A flower to brighten! dawn to bless!

As to the future, think not of it:
  Heaven's paths are darkling, life's affright.
Ah! what makes man that he should love it?
  A little sound in deep midnight.

Our lot is harsh, is all we see.
  Child, often the bright eye that bears
And scatters most of light and glee .
  Bears also and sheddeth most of tears!

You, in whose small soul naught doth seem
  To dwell, have all: bright joy, bright wile,
Sweet innocence which maketh dream,
  Rapt ignorance which maketh smile.

You have, white lily from the wind
  Saved, little heart which small dreams bless,
That calm joy of the infant mind,
  Reflect from mother's happiness.

Your candor makes you beautiful.
  Give me before all other fire
Your deep blue eyes aye wonderful
  With light that makes man's heart beat higher.

For you no sorrows, no pale hours:
  At home you are the cherished pet;
In summer you run among the flowers,
  In winter the hearth make merrier yet.

Sweet poesy, bright bird of the skies,
    Near to you, child, still flutters wings;
Its light is in your mother's eyes,
In your father's thought its murmurings.

Have heed of this swift time so sweet!
    Live, live!   False joy is soon away;
Each of us sighing at your feet
    Hath had bright dawn to somber day.

As one prays ere his steps be gone,
    Let me now bless thee, spirit mild.
Angel, thou'lt wear a martyr's crown—
    Thou must be woman, dearest child!

————

GOD, WHOSE GIFTS IN GRACIOUS FLOOD

God, whose gifts in gracious flood
    Unto all who seek are sent,
Only asks you to be good,
    And is content.

So the world, where all things are
    Sparkling, yet does naught ignite,
Only asks you to be fair,
    And finds delight.

And my heart, in the sweet shade
    Of two beauteous eyes steeped o'er,
Only asks if you be glad,
    And nothing more.

IN THE CEMETERY OF ——

THE crowd still living, laughs, on folly set—
For weal or woe, for better or for worse;
The silent dead, the dead whom they forget,
See me the dreamer, and with me converse.

In me they know the solitary man,
The pilgrim sage who through the forest
wends—
The soul that finds (life's sorrows wont to scan)
That all in grief begins, in quiet ends.

They've seen my pensive look, my drooping
head,
As 'mong the crosses and the tombs I stood ·
Upon the fallen leaves have heard me tread,
Have seen me watch the shades that haunt
the wood.

They understand the truths my words have told,
Far more than you who live in noise and
strife;
The hymns which doth my lyric soul enfold
To you mere songs, to them with tears are
rife.

Though men forget them, Nature still is theirs.
And in death's garden, where we all shall
meet,
Calm dawn an aspect more celestial bears,
The lilies purer seem, the birds more sweet.

'Tis there I live! and there white roses pick;
  Repair the tombs, neglected long, and rent.
I come and go through branches dark and
      thick,
  The dead my footsteps hear, and are content.

There, too, I dream. In that field slumber
      furled,
  Roving, I see with the keen eyes of thought,
My soul transformed into a magic world,
  Mysterious glass of all, by Nature wrought.

I see not, yet behold strange insects fly,
  Boughs indistinct, shapes, hues, around me
      play;
There, resting on the stones that broken lie,
  I dazzling visions have of flower and ray.

The ideal dream which fills my eyelids there
  Floats a bright veil between the earth and
      me.
There my ungrateful doubts melt into prayer;
  Standing at first, I end on bended knee.

As to the hollow in the rock doth come,
  To sip a drop of dew, the humble dove,
So my proud soul, in shadow of the tomb,
  Would drink a little faith and hope and love.

A NIGHT IN JUNE

In summer — daylight fled — where flowers
abound,
  The fields their luscious fragrance pour afar;
With half-closed eyes, ears scarce awake to
sound
  Slumbering, our minds not all unconscious
are.
The stars more pure shine through the shadowy
skies,
  Uncertain twilight tints th' eternal vault;
Dawn, soft and pale, waiting its hour to rise,
  Seems all night long on heaven's low ridge to
halt.

THE POOL AND THE SOUL

As in some stagnant pool by forest-side,
In human souls two things are oft descried—
The sky, which tints the surface of the pool
With all its rays, and all its shadows cool;
The basin next, where gloomy, dark, and deep,
Through slime and mud black reptiles vaguely
creep.

A MEETING

WHEN to the youngest he his alms had cast,
Musing, he stopped to see them.   A long fast
Had thinned their cheeks the sun and wind em-
    browned.
They sat all four together on the ground,
Then having shared, as angels might have done,
A morsel of black bread from gutters won,
They eat, but with a look of woe so deep,
To see them must have made all women weep.
'Tis they are lost, in earth's vast crowded space—
Four children all alone, the world to face;
No father, mother; not a barn, a shed
For shelter; with bare feet the road they tread,
All save the last, who limped, poor little thing,
In shoes old and too large, and tied with string.
In ditches all night through they often sleep;
How cold they are at morn, when chill winds
    sweep,
When the trees, shivering at the lark's first cry,
Make a black profile 'gainst the clear pale sky'
Their hands, which God made pink, now red
    remain.
Sundays they seek the hamlet for vile gain :
The little one, from illness pale and lean,
Sings songs unfit, not knowing what they mean,
To make (poor child, alas! to tears akin)
Some foul hoar villain laugh, who haunts the
    inn.

So is the pot-house merry made, and thence
To their sharp hunger thrown some paltry
    pence—
The alms of hell, designed sin's perquisite,
The hideous coin on which the fiend has spit.
And then to eat behind some hedge they go,
Hidden, and trembling more than fawn or doe,
For oft they're beaten, always chased away.
'Tis thus, poor innocents, condemned each day,
Beneath my walls and yours they famished
    stray,
As chance directs; the eldest leads the way.

Then he, the dreamer, turned his gaze on high,
And naught but calm warm ether meets his
    eye;
The bounteous sun, air full of golden wings,
From the blue vault the sweet soft peace that
    springs;
The joys, the shouts, that Nature's triumph
    swell,
Down from the sky-birds on the children fell.

TO LAURA, DUCHESS D'A.

SINCE were their souls too mean to comprehend
    That after so great splendors, power and
        pride,
Duty and honor called on France to lend
    A grave, wherein thy coffin might abide;

Since they felt not that she who, dauntless still,
  Dared glory, praise, and ruffian knaves con-
    found, •
Has right to sleep upon the holy hill,
  Has right to sleep where heroes rest around:

Of our great battles, since the memory
  Burns not within them, like a sacred flame;
Since they are void of heart and sympathy,
  Who could refuse (small boon) the tomb you
    claim—

'Tis mine to sing an expiatory song;
  Mine, on my knees, our sorrow to rehearse;
To me to guard thy memory doth belong,
  And to embalm in sweet and mournful verse.

This time, 'tis mine to shelter and defend
  Death 'gainst its comrade, pale Forgetfulness;
With scattered roses, mine thine urn to tend,
  To crown thy name with laurels—and redress.

Since fools heap insults, now thou'rt sunk to
    rest,
  Upon thy brow, by Cæsar glorious made,
'Tis mine, whose hand thine own in friendship
    prest,
  To whisper, "I am near: be not afraid!"

For I my mission have. Armed with my lyre,
  Full of fierce hymns which would their wrath
    declare,
Guarding the glories, I, of the Empire,
  Resolved that none these to attack shall dare.

Its memories in thy faithful heart were stored,
  When adverse skies spread o'er us Sorrow's
    night.
On noble wrongs thy noble spirit soared,
  Oft with an eagle's eye, with angels' flight.

Brave 'neath thy woes, of ours compassionate,
  Woman! to storms and hostile strife a prey,
Thou never didst their baseness imitate,
  Nor trod to safety's port by coward's way.

Thou glorious muse, and (though inglorious) I,
  Have each our lives this mandate laid upon:
A steadfast knot which each to each doth tie
  The hero's widow, and the soldier's son.

Hence in this Babel, I for evermore
  Each scrap of our scorned flag shall kiss and
    save.
Unto the emperor I bade France restore
  His column, and to thee to grant the grave.

I WAS ALWAYS A LOVER

I was always a lover of soft-winged things.
When a child, allured by bird-murmurings,
I sought them, and took the small sweets from
    the leaves.
And at first my timid delight in them weaves
Reed-cages, and lo! they got plumes 'mong
    green moss.
Later I threw wide the lattice, but loss

Sustained not; thev flew not—or, if they *did* fly,
But went to the woods and came back at my cry.
A fond dove and I cooed together love's name:
Now I have knowledge, men's spirits to tame.

THE MARBLE FAUN

HE seemed to shiver, for the wind was keen:
'Twas a poor statue underneath a mass
Of leafless branches, with a blackened back
And a green foot—an isolated Faun
In old deserted park, who, bending forward,
Half-merged himself in the entangled boughs,
Half in his marble settings.   He was there,
Pensive, and bound to earth; and, as all things
Devoid of movement, he was there—forgotten.

Trees were around him, whipped by icy blasts—
Gigantic chestnuts, without leaf or bird,
And, like himself, grown old in that same place.
Through the dark network of their undergrowth,
Pallid his aspect; and the earth was brown.
Starless and moonless, a rough winter's night
Was letting down her lappets o'er the mist.
This, nothing more: old Faun, dull sky, dark
    wood.

Poor, helpless marble, how I've pitied it!—
Less often man, the harder of the two.
So, then, without a word that might offend
His ear deformed—for well the marble hears

The voice of thought—I said to him · "You hail
From the gay amorous age.   O Faun, what saw
 you
When you were happy?   Were you of the Court?

"Speak to me, comely Faun, as you would speak
To tree or zephyr or untrodden grass.
Have you, O Greek, O mocker of old days
Have you not sometimes with that oblique eye
Winked at the Farnese Hercules?   Alone,
Have you, O Faun, considerately turned
From side to side when counsel-seekers came,
And now advised as shepherd, now as satyr?
Have you sometimes, upon this very bench
Seen at midday Vincent de Paul instilling
Grace into Gondi?   Have you ever thrown
That searching glance on Louis with Fontange,
On Anne with Buckingham; and did they not
Start, with flushed cheeks, to hear your laugh
 ring forth
From corner of the wood?   Was your advice
As to the thyrsis or the ivy asked,
When, in grand ballet of fantastic form,
God Phœbus, or God Pan, and all his court,
Turned the fair head of the proud Montespan,
Calling her Amaryllis?   La Fontaine,
Flying the courtiers' ears of stone, came he,
Tears on his eyelids, to reveal to you
The sorrows of his nymphs of Vaux?   What
 said
Boileau to you—to you, O lettered Faun,
Who once with Virgil, in the eclogue, held
That charming dialogue?   Say, have you seen

Young beauties sporting on the sward?   Have
    you
Been honored with a sight of Molière
In dreamy mood?   Has he perchance, at eve,
When here the thinker homeward went—has he,
Who, seeing souls all naked, could not fear
Your nudity, in his inquiring mind
Confronted you with Man?''

Under the thickly tangled branches thus
Did I speak to him; he no answer gave.

I shook my head, and moved myself away;
Then from the copses, and from secret caves
Hid in the wood, methought a ghostly voice
Came forth and woke an echo in my soul,
As in the hollow of an amphora.
"Imprudent poet," thus it seemed to say,
"What dost thou here?   Leave the forsaken Fauns
In peace beneath their trees!
Dost thou not know,
Poet, that ever it is impious deemed
In desert spots where drowsy shades repose—
Though love itself might prompt thee—to shake
    down
The moss that hangs from ruined centuries,
And with the vain noise of thine ill timed words
To mar the recollections of the dead?''

Then to the gardens all enwrapped in mist
I hurried, dreaming of the vanished days;
And still behind me—hieroglyph obscure
Of antique alphabet—the lonely Faun
Held to his laughter, through the falling night.

I went my way; but yet—in saddened spirit
Pondering on all that had my vision crossed:
Leaves of old summers, fair ones of old time—
Through all, at distance, would my fancy see
In the woods statues: shadows in the past!

L'ANNÉE TERRIBLE.—1872

TO LITTLE JEANNE

You've lived a year, then, yesterday, sweet
  child,
Prattling thus happily! So fledgelings wild
New-hatched in warmer nest 'neath sheltering
  bough,
Chirp merrily to feel their feathers grow.
Your mouth's a rose, Jeanne! In these volumes
  grand
Whose pictures please you—while I trembling
  stand
To see their big leaves tattered by your hand—
Are noble lines, but nothing half your worth,
When all your tiny frame rustles with mirth
To welcome me. No work of author wise
Can match the thought half springing to your
  eyes,
And your dim reveries, unfettered, strange,
Regarding man with all the boundless range
Of angel innocence. Methinks, 'tis clear
That God's not far, Jeanne, when I see you
  here.

Ah, twelve months old! 'Tis quite an age, and
    brings
Grave moments, though your soul to rapture
    clings.
You're at that hour of life most like to heaven,
When present joy no cares, no sorrows leaven·
When man no shadow feels: if fond caress
Round parent twines, children the world possess.
Your waking hopes, your dreams of mirth and
    love
From Charles to Alice, father to mother, rove;
No wider range of view your heart can take
Than what her nursing and his bright smiles
    make.
They two alone on this your opening hour
Can gleams of tenderness and gladness pour—
They two: none else, Jeanne! Yet 'tis just;
    and I,
Poor grandsire, dare but to stand humbly by.
You come, I go: though gloom alone my right,
Blest be the destiny which gives you light.

Your fair-haired brother George and you be-
    side
Me play—in watching you is all my pride;
And all I ask (by countless sorrows tried)
The grave, o'er which in shadowy form may
    show
Your cradles gilded by the morning's glow.

Pure new-born wonderer! your infant life
Strange welcome found, Jeanne, in this time of
    strife.

Like wild bee humming through the woods your
     play,
And baby smiles have dared a world at bay;
Your tiny accents lisp their gentle charms
To mighty Paris clashing mighty arms.
Ah, when I see you, child, and when I hear
You sing, or try, with low voice whispering
     near,
And touch of fingers soft, my grief to cheer,
I dream this darkness where the tempests
     groan
Trembles, and passes with half-uttered moan;
For though these hundred towers of Paris bend,
Though close as foundering ship her glory's
     end,
Though rocks the universe which we defend;
Still to great cannon on our ramparts piled,
God sends his blessing by a little child.

CONTENTMENT

LET no one ask me how it came to pass;
   It seems that I am happy, that to me
A livelier emerald sparkles in the grass,
   A purer sapphire melts into the sea.

WHAT DICTATES THE BOOK

My soul seems, in this frightful season of time
Thronged by the monstrous jostling the sublime,
A plain given up to every wandering tread,
Ceaselessly trampled by deeds grand or dread.
This book of mine's dictated day by day
By the hour that roars, then moans its life away.
The weeks of the Awful Year are hydras dire,
Hell-born of fire to be consumed by fire;
Onward with blazing eyes they all must roll,
Leaving the burning grip upon my soul.
Upon my verse, wan, wild for pity or wrath,
Th' imprint one sees upon a serpent's path.
Should one regard my spirit now, he'd see
Dark signs thereon engraven countlessly
Of all these days of horror, doubt, defiance,
As 'twere a desert trampled o'er by lions.

SEDAN

Toulon was naught; Sedan is more! The
wretch
O'er whom does logic doom its trammels stretch,
Slave of his crimes—given up with bandaged
eyes
To the black haps which played with him at dice,
Dreamer—is whelmed in endless infamy;
The far-off formidable gaze on high,

Which ne'er looks off from crime, marked all
    his way.
God pushed the tyrant—worm and ghost to-
    day—
Into a gloom that history shudders o'er,
And which for none he opened up before;
There, in the gulf's worst chasm, was he cast:
The Judge all that was prophesied, surpassed.

That man once chanced to dream: "I reign, 'tis
    true!
But men despise me; they must fear me too.
I, in my turn, will rule the world; I'm quite
My uncle's equal. Terror is my right.
No Austerlitz, yet my Brumaire I have.
For him both Machiavel and Homer slave,
And both kept busy with the task he set;
I want but Machiavel—I've Galifet;
Morny was mine, Rouher, Devienne, remain.
Madrid, Vienna, Lisbon, though unta'en,
Yet Dresden, Munich, Naples I shall take;
St. Andrew's cross from off the ocean rake,
And that old Albion to subjection bring.
A robber's naught, unless a conquering king!
I will be great, a pirate, slaves will own—
Mitered Mastai, Abdul on his throne,
The Czar in bear-skin robe and ermined crown.
Since I with shells Montmartre have battered
    down,
I can take Prussia—'tis as sharp to win
By siege Tortoni, as besiege Berlin.
Who took a bank, may also take Mayence·
Stamboul and Petersburg are mere pretense.

Pius, Emmanuel, both at daggers drawn,
Like two he-goats, fierce fighting on a lawn;
England and Ireland at each other rail
And Spain on Cuba pours an iron hail;
Joseph and William at each other's hair—
Mock Attila, sham Cæsar—fiercely tear;
And I, once down-at-heel and tippler known,
Shall be the arbiter of every throne.
This glory I shall reach without a blow.
To be supreme, the mightiest here below,
From false Napoleon seem the true Charlemagne,
'Tis fine! How do the trick? Ask banker
    Magne
To advance Lebœuf some money, then look out
(Thus Haroun and his vizier stole about),
When all men sleep and streets deserted lie,
And quickly try the chance, and surely I
May cross the Rhine, who crossed the Rubicon.
Garlands and flowers shall Pietri throw me down.
Magnan is dead, but Frossard I retain;
St. Arnaud's missing, still I have Bazaine.
That Bismarck's but a mountebank, is plain;
I think I play a part as well as he.
Up to this time, chance has complied with me—
Has been my·'complice. Fraud for wife I have;
Coward, I've conquered; shone although a
    knave.
Forward! I've Paris, therefore all mankind.
All things smile on me, why then lag behind?
I want but doublets, and my fortune's made.
Let me go on, since Fortune is a jade,
The world is mine; I choose to govern all;
'Neath juggler's cup I hold the starry ball.

I cheated France, now let us Europe cheat.
My cloak, December! Night, my hiding-sheet!
Eagles are gone; I've naught but buzzards now.
'Tis night: I'll use it, and try anyhow."

Full day on Rome, Vienna, London, lies,
And, save that man, all opened wide their eyes.
Berlin watched silent, smiling with delight;
As he was blind he fancied it was night.
All saw the light, he only saw the shade.

Alas! no count of time, place, number made,
Groping unhelped, trusting to destiny,
And having darkness for his sole ally.
This suicide France's proud armies took—
Which honor never yet, nor fame, forsook—

And without arms, bread, chiefs, or general,
To the gulf's lowest depth conducted all;
Tranquil the whole into the trap he led.
"Where go you?" cried the tomb.
                              "Who knows?" he said.

  .   .   .   .

Agincourt smiles, henceforward Ramillies,
Trafalgar, shall our hours of sorrow please;
Poitiers is no grief, Blenheim's no disgrace,
Crecy no field which makes us veil our face,
Black Rosbach almost seems a victory.
This! France, thy hideous spot in history—
Sedan! Death-name, which all has darkened
        o'er,
Spit forth! so never to pronounce it more.

  .   .   .   .

Fierce was the strife! The carnage large and dire
Gave to the combatants a glance of fire.

Shrieking, the fell Furies at distance stood;
In a dark cloud, all spattered o'er with blood,
Mitrailleuses, mortars, cannons, belch their war.
Ravens, those busy workers, come from far;
Banquets are slaughter, massacre a feast.
Rage filled the gloom, and spread from breast to
    breast.
All Nature part in the fierce battle takes,
From man who maddens, to the tree that shakes;
The fatal field itself seemed frenzied o'er;
One is repulsed, one driven on before.
Now France, now Germany successful cope;
All either had of death the tragic hope,
Or hideous joy of killing. No man shrunk;
All with the acrid scent of blood were drunk.
None yield; each this the fatal hour knows.
That seed an arm of fearful power sows;
Bullets rained down upon the darkened sod;
The wounded groaned, the nearest on them trod;
The hoarse-mouthed cannon on the _mêlée_ blew
A vast, thick smoke, which on the breezes flew.
Country, devotion, fame, their thoughts engage,
And duty's call, beneath their desperate rage.
Sudden—in all this mist, 'mid thunder's breath,
In the vast gloom where laughs imagined death;
In clash of epic shocks, and in the hell
Of brass and copper which on iron fell;
The crash, the crush, of hurtling shell and bomb,
In rain and rave of that wild hecatomb;
While the harsh clarions sound their dismal cry,
The while our soldiers strive and proudly try
To mate the deeds of their great ancestors—
A shudder through the haggard standards pours;

While waiting the decree of destiny
(All bleed, fight bravely, strive, or nobly die),
They heard the monstrous words, "I wish to
    live!"

The cannons are struck dumb; no longer strive
The blood-drunk hosts—the abysmal word was
    said,

And the black eagle waits with claws outspread.

PARIS SLANDERED

THE gloomy night, to hate the dawn is wont:
Th' Athenian seems to Vandal an affront.
Paris, while they attack, they think it best
To make their ambush look like an arrest.
Pedant helps soldier; both together vie
To asperse th' heroic city.   Calumny,
Mingled with shells, in the bombardment rains,
The soldier kills; and lies the pleader feigns.
Your morals, your religion they accuse,
And insults heap their murder to excuse.
They slander that they may assassinate.
City and people, as a senate great,
Fight! draw the sword, O city of the light
Which fosters art, defends the cotter's right!
Let, O proud home of man's equality!
Howl round thee the foul hordes of bigotry—
Black props of throne and altar; hypocrites,
Who in all ages have proscribed the lights:

Who guard all gods against th' inquiring mind;
Whose screech in every history we find
At Thebes, Mycenæ, Delphi, Memphis, Rome—
Like bark of unclean dogs from distance come.

FROM THE INVESTED WALLS OF PARIS

BRIGHT white the west, dense black the eastern
    sky:
    As some invisible arm from heaven let fall,
To serve eve's columns for a canopy,
    O'er this horizon a shroud, o'er that a pall.

Night shut in earth, as 'twere a prison cold.
    Last plaint of bird, last light of leaf, were
        quenched.
Descending, again I looked toward heaven; be-
        hold!
    In the low west a bright blade shone, blood-
        drenched.

That made me muse of some vast duel dread,
    Fought by a god matched 'gainst some giant-
        birth—
The awful sword o' the vanquished, one had
        said,
    Bloodied with battle, fallen from heaven to
        earth!

CAPITULATION

THUS greatest nations to their fall descend—
'Tis in miscarriage all their labors end;
"Was it for this," th' indignant people say,
"We did all night on the high bastions stay?
Were we for this unconquered, lofty, stark,
And of the Prussian missiles stood the mark?
Was it for this, we heroes, martyrs were,
And more and fiercer war than Tyre bare;
Than Corinth or Byzantium more endured·
For this, for five long months, have been im-
        mured
By those black furtive Teutons, in whose eyes
The gloomy stupor of weird forests lies?
For this dug mines, and borne the strife im-
        mense,
Broke bridges, famine braved, and pestilence;
Did trenches make, fix piles, and towers build,
O France! and with the seed of slaughter filled
The grave—of battles the black granary?
For this did storm and shot each day defy?"

High Heavens! after such tests, such noble
        deeds
By Paris wrought, which uncomplaining bleeds;
After vast hopes, and expectations high
Of the proud town panting for victory,
Which dashing 'gainst the cannon iron knit
Appeared its walls to champ, as horse its bit;

Where valor greater grew, new woes to meet;
Where children, shelled while running in the
    street,
Picked up the shells and cannon-balls in sport;
When not one single citizen fell short
(Three hundred thousand for the battle steeled) —
Their officers th' unconquered city yield!
With your devotion, fury, pride of heart,
And courage, they have played the coward's
    part,
People! And history shall loathe and blame
Such glory, tarnished by so deep a shame.

THE SICK CHILD

If still your little face this pallor has
    In our close air defiled;
If you within my fatal shadow pass—
    I, aged; you, a child;

If of our days, I, tangled, see the chain—
    I who on bended knee
Watch you, and long that I by death was
    ta'en,
    And you from danger free;

If still your thin frail hands let through the
    day,
    If in your cot you lie
Shivering—you seem like a small bird to
    stay
    For wings, that you may fly.

Root on our earth to take, if you appear
　　But for a little space.
If, Jeanne, your eyes go wandering here
　　　and there
　　In this mysterious place;

If you are rosy, gay, and strong no more;
　　If, musing, you are sad;
If after you, you do not shut the door
　　By which you entrance had;

If, as a lovely girl, I may not see
　　That well and bright you grow,
And glad; but seem a little soul to be,
　　Which is in haste to go—

I deem that here, where swaddling clothes
　　　and shroud
　　Oft close together dwell,
You came to flit: and angel art allowed
　　Me, too, to take as well.

———

BEFORE THE CONCLUSION OF THE TREATY

IF this foul war we ended see,
　　And grant all Prussia longs to get,
Then like a glass our France would be,
　　Upon a pothouse table set—

You empty it, and then you break!
Our haughty country is no more.
Oh, grief, that shame should overtake
Where only honor lived of yore!

Black morrow, with dismay for text!
All dregs we drink; on ashes feed.
The eagles gone, there follow next
The vultures; these do hawks succeed.

Two provinces now torn away—
Metz poisoned, Strasburg crucified;
Sedan, deserter in the fray,
A brand on France that will abide.

There lives in souls degenerate
Base love of loathly happiness—
Pride cast away; they cultivate
The growth, the increase, of disgrace

Our ancient splendor stained, belied;
Our mighty wars dishonored now·
The country mazed and stupefied,
Unused to live with lowered brow·

The foeman in our citadels;
Attila's shadow o'er us thrown—·
The swallow to its fellow tells,
"This is not France that we have
    known."

Her mouth full of the foul Bazaine!
Renown, with slow and broken wing,
Does with unwholesome slaver stain
The trump that erst did nobly ring.

Brethren alone they dare to fight.
Bayard! thy name no longer lives;
They murder now, to hide from sight
That lately they were fugitives.

Black night mounts up on every brow,
And not a soul dares soar on high;
Heaven does itself our shame avow,
Since we refuse to seek the sky.

Chill hearts are here, and darkness deep;
People from people separate;
All wide apart and hostile keep,
And love is dead, and turned to hate.

Prussia and France are foemen sworn;
That host is all with hatred fired;
Our dark eclipse their joyful mourn
Our tomb by all of them desired.

Shipwreck! To mighty deeds good-by'
Deceived, deceiving all is made;
"The cowards!" to our flag they cry,
And to our cannon, "They're afraid!"

Our pride, our hopes, departed all—
A shroud on history fallen is.
O God! permit not France to fall
In gulf of such a peace as this.

TOYS AND TRAGEDY.

THE STRUGGLE

'TIS angry ignorance to pity those
Who still their eyes to truth's bright radiance
　　close;
And, friend, why care?　Honor with us we see.
Pity those rulers who on bended knee
Sign the vile peace which France doth gripe
　　and rend;
Let their insane ingratitude descend
In history with your contempt and mine.
Jesus Himself their malice would malign;
Paul a fierce democrat they would have named,
And Socrates as a mere quack defamed.
They're made so their blear eyes the daylight
　　fear—
The fault not theirs, at Naples, Rome, or here.
Throughout, 'tis natural these souls perverse
As soldiers, envy you; as priests, should curse—
The first being beaten, and unmasked the last.
The ice which by our quays this winter past
Pell-mell, and all things cold and gloomy made,
Yet drifting quickly melted in the shade,
Was not more hateful, nor more vain than this.
You who of old (as heaven-sent warriors mav)
Freed cities, without armies and alone,
Let their vile clamors at your head be thrown.
What matters it!　Clasp we our hands anew—
I, the old Frenchman; the old Roman you.
Let us go hence this place, unmeet and vain,
And let us each our lofty cliffs regain,

Where, if we're hissed, at least 'tis bv the sea;
Come, let the lightning our insulter be—
Furv not base, grief worthy of the brave ·
True gulfs—and quit their slaver for the wave.

TOYS AND TRAGEDY

IN later years they'll tell you grandpapa
Adored his little darlings; for them did
His utmost just to pleasure them and mar
No moments with a frown or growl amid
Their rosy rompings; that he loved them so
(Though men have called him bitter, cold,
    and stern)
That in the famous winter when the snow
Covered poor Paris, he went, old and worn,
To buy them toys, despite the falling shells,
At which, like they, laughed Punch, with
    all his bells.

IN THE CIRCUS

THE southern lion saw the Polar bear
Rush at him, gnash, and, full of fiery glare,
Attack him, growling worse than Nubian wind.
The lion said, "You idiot, never mind;
We're in the circus, and you fight with me.
What for? That low-browed fellow do you see?

That's Nero—Roman Emperor, so it haps.
You fight for him, bleed, and he laughs and
    claps.
Brother, in the wide world we ne'er were foes,
And heaven alike o'er each its mantle throws.
You see above no fewer stars than I.
With us, what wants that master set on high?
He's pleased—but we? We by his order fight:
His business is to laugh, and ours to bite.
He makes us kill each other; while, good sooth,
Brother, my claw gives answer to your tooth,
He's there upon his throne, with gaze intent,
Our pangs his sport! Our spheres are different.
Brother, when we our life-blood shed in streams,
To him, in purple clad, it harmless seems.
Come, dolt, set on! my claws prepared you
    see:
But still, I think and say, we fools shall be
In internecine strife to spend our power,
And wiser 'twere the emperor to devour!

BRUTE WAR

Toiler sans eyes, dull-brained Penelope,
  Cradler of chaos, powerless to create;
War, whom the clash of iron fires to glee,
  The furious blast of clarions makes elate;
Quaffer of blood; foul hag that to thy feast
  Lur'st men and madden'st them with vile de-
    light;

Cloud, swollen with thunder north, south, west,
    and east,
Fulfilled with rage darker than darkest night;
Vast madness, that for swords keen lightnings
    wieldest:
What is thy use, dire birth of hellish race,
If, while thou ruinest sin, crime thou upbuildest,
    Setting the monster i' the beast's pride of
      place;
    If with thine awful darkness thou dost
      smother
    One emperor, but to yield earth thence
      another?

AT THE BARRICADE

Upon a barricade thrown 'cross the street
Where patriot's blood with felon's stains one's
    feet,
Ta'en with grown men, a lad aged twelve, or
    less!
"Were you among them—you?" He answered:
    "Yes."
"Good!" said the officer. "When comes your
    turn,
You'll be shot too." The lad sees lightnings
    burn—
Stretched 'neath the wall his comrades one by
    one:
Then says to the officer, "First let me run
And take this watch home to my mother, sir?"

"You want to escape?" "No, I'll come back."
"What fear
These brats have! Where do you live?" "By
the well, below;
I'll return quickly if you let me go."
"Be off, young scamp!" Off went the boy.
"Good joke!"
And here from all a hearty laugh outbroke,
And with this laugh the dying mixed their
moan.
But the laugh suddenly ceased, when, paler
grown,
'Midst them the lad appeared, and breathlessly
Stood upright 'gainst the wall with· "Here am
I."
Dull death was shamed; the officer said, "Be
free!"

Child, I know not, in all this agony
Where good and ill as with one blast of hell
Are blent, *thy* part; but this I know right well,
That thy young soul's a hero-soul sublime.
Gentle and brave, thou trod'st, despite all crime,
Two steps—one toawrd thy mother, one toward
death.
For the child's deeds the grown man answereth;
No fault was thine to march where others led.
But glorious aye that child who chose instead
Of flight that lured to life, love, freedom, May,
The somber wall 'neath which slain comrades
lay!
Glory on thy young brow imprints her kiss.
In Hellas old, sweetheart, thou hadst, I wis,

After some deathless fight to win or save,
Been hailed by comrades bravest of the brave;
Hadst smiling in the holiest ranks been found,
Haply by some Æschylean verse bright-crowned!
On brazen disks thy name had been engraven;
One of those godlike youths who, 'neath blue
　　heaven,
Passing some well whereo'er the willow droops
What time some virgin 'neath her pitcher stoops
Brimmed for her herds a-thirst, brings to her
　　eyes
A long, long look of awed yet sweet surmise.

TO THOSE WHO TALK ABOUT FRA-
TERNITY

WHEN we are conquerors, we'll see; till then
The feeling fitting grief is fierce disdain:
Best suits defeat the gloomy downcast eye.
Free, we spread light; enslaved, we prophesy.
We're burked, and 'twixt us twain no love can
　　dwell.
The ruin of the invader I foretell.
'Tis proper pride, in those who feel the chain,
Hatred alone for shelter to retain;
To love the Germans, that will come, what time
Our victory makes to love no longer crime.
Peace to proclaim is always false and vain
In those who, vanquished, have not vengeance
　　ta'en.

Let's wait the time when we the road com-
mand—
When 'neath our feet; then hold them out the
hand.
I can but bleed so long as France doth weep;
For fitter time all talk of concord keep.
Fraternity stammered out, and meant but half,
But makes the foe his shoulders shrug and
laugh;
The offer to be friends, and rancor stay,
To-morrow may be fine, but base to-day.

PAST PARTICIPLE OF THE VERB
TROPCHOIR

PAST participle of *tropchoir*—man fraught
With virtues numberless, whose sum is naught;
Brave, pious soldier, useless for attack,
Not a bad cannon—but too apt to back;
Christian, upright, who twofold merit has,
Of serving both his country and the mass.
I do you justice. Why, then, at me carp?
You make on me, in style oblique and sharp,
Assaults, which, if on Prussia made, had told
During the Prussian siege, and Russian cold.
Being an old man, I bore not arms. Confest!
Glad to be shut in Paris with the rest;
And sometimes, while did shot and bullets fall,
Would in my turn mount guard upon the wall:
Cried, "Here!" though old, and by decree of
Fate
Useless, yet did I not capitulate!

In your hands laurels turned to nettles be;
You make your only sorties against me.
Of them in that bad siege we thought you slack:
Well, we were wrong—for me you kept them
    back.
You, who to cross the main were never known,
Why fly at me, since I left you alone?
Why should my blue cloth coat your eyes dis-
    please,
Or my *kepi* disturb your chaplet's ease?

Cold, famine, five long months we underwent,
And dread of worse.   And are you not content?
Brave, faithful, we ne'er harassed you at all.
Say, if you please, you're a great general;
But to dash through the gulf, through foes to
    break,
To sound the charge, through fire your host to
    take,
Barra, the subaltern, I covet more.

See Garibaldi, from Caprera's shore,
Kleber at Cairo, or on Venice walls
Manin.   Be calm!   Great Paris dies and falls
Because you lacked not heart but faith.   Alas!
On you will history this sentence pass:
France, thanks to him, fought with but half her
    power
In those great days, in strife's decisive hour;
The land which wounds, death, foes could ne'er
    subdue,
Marched with Gambetta, halted with Trochu.

THE SORTIE

THE chill dawn glimmered, wan for night's de-
　　feat.
A troop defiled in order through the street;
I followed, by that rumor vast drawn on
Of men's feet trampling in strong unison.
Citizens were they, marching for the fight.
Pure warriors!　In the ranks, less as to height,
But by the heart compeer, the child with pride
Held by the hand his father, by whose side,
Bearing her husband's rifle, marched the wife.
Still, as of yore, our Gallic girls in strife
Are proud their warriors' glittering arms to bear,
If one beard Cæsar, or brave Atilla.
What next?　The child laughs; those dark eyes
　　of yours,
Mother, are dry.　Paris defeat endures;
But all her children are on this agreed,
That, save by shame, no people's shamed indeed,
That their dead sires will blush not, come what
　　may,
So Paris die that France may live for aye.
Honor we keep; for the rest we care not—we.
So forward!　On pale brows inscribed we see,
'Bove eyes aflame, Faith, Courage, and Starva-
　　tion.
Onward these warriors of a glorious nation
March, 'neath her banner, torn, but undefiled.
With the battalion mingle wife and child,

To leave it only at the city-gates.
These men devoted, and their warrior-mates
Sing.   Paris bleeds for the whole human race.
An ambulance passes; of all tyrants base
One muses, whose least whim makes rivers red
Flow from out veins of victor and vanquishèd.
The hour draws nigh; to the sortie drums beat,
While troops high-hearted pour from street on
        street;
All hasten.   To the leaguer woe this morn!
Ambushes! but all snares one holds in scorn,
Knowing the valiant, vanquished thus, acclaimed
Glorious of all men, while the victor's shamed.
At th' walls they arrive, concentrate; suddenly
Adrift on the wind a wreath of smoke we see:
Halt!   'Tis the signal-gun!   Another!   Lo,
Through massed battalions runs a mighty throe!
The moment's come; the gates are opened wide;
Trumpets, speak loud!   Yon low green plains
        divide
From us the woods where lurks the foe unseen;
The horizon stretches motionless, serene,
Slumberous, insidious, with dire flames replete.
Listen, low words: "Adieu!—my rifle, sweet!"
And wives, heart-broken, brow where naught's
        amiss,
Give up the rifles, sacred with love's kiss.

MOURNING

CHARLES, Charles, my son! hast thou, then,
        quitted me?
    Must all fade, naught endure?
Hast vanished in that radiance, clear for thee,
    But still for us obscure?

My sunset lingers, boy; thy morn declines!
    Sweet mutual love we've known;
For man, alas! plans, dreams, and smiling
        twines
    With others' souls his own.

He cries, "This has no end!" pursues his way.
    He soon is downward bound ·
He lives, he suffers: in his grasp one day
    Mere dust and ashes found.

I've wandered twenty years in distant lands,
    With sore heart forced to stay;
Why fell the blow, Fate only understands.
    God took my home away.

To-day one daughter and one son remain
    Of all my goodly show:
Wellnigh in solitude my dark hours wane.
    God takes my children now.

Linger, ye two still left me! Though decays
    Our nest, our hearts remain;
In gloom of death your mother silent prays,
    I in this life of pain.

Martyr of Zion! holding thee in sight,
    I'll drain this cup of gall,
And scale with step resolved that dangerous
    height,
    Which rather seems a fall.

Truth is sufficient guide; no more man needs
    Than end so nobly shown.
Mourning, but brave, I march where duty leads;
    I seek the vast unknown.

———

TO HIS ORPHAN GRANDCHILDREN

I FEEL thy presence, Charles. Sweet martyr!
    down
    In earth, where men decay,
I search, and see from cracks which rend thy
    tomb
    Burst out pale morning's ray.

Close linked are bier and cradle: here the dead,
    To charm us, live again.
Kneeling, I mourn, when on my threshold
    sounds
    Two little children's strain.

George, Jeanne, sing on! George, Jeanne, un-
    conscious play!
    Your father's form recall,
Now darkened by his somber shade, now gilt
    By beams that wandering fall.

O knowledge! what thy use, did we not know
    Death holds no more the dead,
But heaven, where, hand in hand, angel and
    star
    Smile at the grave we dread?--

A heaven which childhood represents on earth.
    Orphans, may God be nigh!--
That God who can your bright steps turn aside
    From darkness, where I sigh.

All joy be yours, though sorrow bows me down!
    To each his fitting wage.
Children, I've passed life's span; and men are
    plagued
    By shadows at that stage.

Hath any done—nay, only half performed—
    The good he might for others?
Hath any conquered hatred, or had strength
    To treat his foes like brothers?

E'en he who's tried his best, hath evil wrought:
    Pain springs from happiness.
My heart has triumphed in defeat, my pulse
    Ne'er quickened at success.

I seemed the greater when I felt the blow:
    The prick gives sense of gain.
Since to make others bleed my courage fails,
    I'd rather bear the pain.

To grow is sad, since evil grows no less;
    Great height is mark for all.
The more I have of branches, more of clustering
    boughs,
    The ghastlier shadows fall.

Thence comes my sadness, though I grant your
    charms:
    Ye are the outbursting
Of the soul in bloom, steeped in the draughts
    Of Nature's boundless spring.

George is the sapling, set in mournful soil;
    Jeanne's folding petals shroud
A mind which trembles at our uproar, yet
    Half longs to speak aloud.

Give, then, my children—lowly, blushing plants,
    Whom sorrow waits to seize—
Free course to instincts, whispering 'mid the
    flowers,
    Like hum of murmuring bees.

Some day you'll find that chaos comes, alas!
    That angry lightning's hurled,
When any cheer the people—Atlas huge,
    Grim bearer of the world!

You'll see that, since our fate is ruled by chance,
    Each man, unknowing, great,
Should frame life so that at some future hour
    Fact and his dreamings meet.

I, too, when death is past, one day shall grasp
    That end I know not now;
And over you will bend me down, all filled
    With dawn's mysterious glow.

I'll learn what means this exile, what this shroud
    Enveloping your prime;
And why the truth and sweetness of one man
    Seem to all others crime.

I'll hear (though midst these dismal boughs you
    sang)
    How came it that for me,
Who every pity feel for every woe,
    So vast a gloom could be.

I'll know why night relentless holds me; why
    So great a pile of doom;
Why endless frost enfolds me, and methinks
    My nightly bed's a tomb;

Why all these battles, all these tears, regrets,
    And sorrows were my share;
And why God's will of me a cypress made,
    When roses bright ye were.

THE TERRIBLE YEAR

THAT dreadful year I gird me to relate,
And now bent o'er my desk I hesitate.
Shall I go further on, or shall I stay?
O France! O grief! to see a star decay.
I feel the blush of rueful shame arise;
Plagues heaped on plagues, and woes on
 agonies.
Still must I on for truth and history;
The age stands at the bar—the witness, I.

THE PAST.

LES VOIX INTERIEURES

CHARITY

"Lo! I am Charity," she cries,
  "Who waketh up before the day;
While yet asleep all Nature lies,
  God bids me rise and go my way."

   .   .   .   .   .

How fair her glorious features shine,
  Whereon the hand of God hath set
An angel's attributes divine,
  With all a woman's sweetness met.

Above the old man's couch of woe
  She bows her forehead, pure and even;
There's nothing fairer here below,
  There's nothing grander up in heaven,

Than when caressingly she stands
  (The cold hearts wakening 'gain their
      beat),
And holds within her holy hands
  The little children's naked feet.

To every den of want and toil
  She goes, and leaves the poorest fed—
Leaves wine and bread and genial oil,
  And hopes that blossom in her tread;

And fire, too—beautiful bright fire,
  That mocks the glowing dawn begun,
Where, having set the blind old sire,
  He dreams he's sitting in the sun.

Then over all the earth she runs,
  And seeks, in the cold mists of life,
Those poor forsaken little ones
  Who droop and weary in the strife.

Ah, most her heart is stirred for them
  Whose foreheads, wrapped in mists ob-
    scure,
Still wear a triple diadem—
  The young, the innocent, the poor.

And they are better far than we,
  And she bestows a worthier meed;
For with the loaf of charity
  She gives the kiss that children need.

She gives, and while they wondering eat
  The tear-steeped bread by love sup-
    plied,
She stretches round them in the street
  Her arm that passers push aside.

If, with raised head and step alert
　She sees the rich man stalking by,
She touches his embroidered skirt,
　And gently shows them where they lie.

She begs for them of careless crowd,
　Of earnest brows and narrow hearts,
That when it hears her cry aloud
　Turns like the ebb-tide and departs.

Oh, miserable he who sings
　Some strain impure, whose numbers fall
Along the cruel wind that brings
　Death to some child beneath his wall.

Oh, strange and sad and fatal thing,
　When, in the rich man's gorgeous hall,
The huge fire on the hearth doth fling
　A light on some great festival,

To see the drunkard smile in state,
　In purple wrapped, with myrtle crowned,
While Jesus lieth at the gate
　With only rags to wrap him round.

———

THE BLINDED BOURBONS

WHO *then* to them had told the Future's story
Or said that France, low bowed before their glory,
　One day would mindful be
Of them and of their mournful fate no more
Than of the wrecks its waters have swept o'er
　The unremembering sea?

That their old Tuileries should see the fall
Of blazons from its high heraldic hall,
    Dismantled, crumbling, prone;
Or that, o'er yon dark Louvre's architrave
A Corsican, as yet unborn, should grave
    An eagle, then unknown?

That gay St. Cloud another lord awaited,
Or that in scenes Le Nôtre's art created
    For princely sport and ease,
Crimean steeds, trampling the velvet glade,
Should browse the bark beneath the stately shade
    Of the great Louis' trees?

TO ALBERT DÜRER

THROUGH ancient forests—where like flowing
    tide
The rising sap shoots vigor far and wide,
Mounting the column of the alder dark
And silv'ring o'er the birch's shining bark—
Hast thou not often, Albert Dürer, strayed
Pond'ring, awestricken, through the half-lit glade,
Pallid and trembling, glancing not behind
From mystic fear that did thy senses bind,
Yet made thee hasten with unsteady pace?
Oh, master grave! whose musings lone we trace
Throughout thy works, we look on reverently.
Amid the gloomy umbrage thy mind's eye
Saw clearly, 'mong the shadows soft yet deep,
The web-toed faun, and Pan the green-eyed
    peep,

Who decked with flowers the cave where thou
    might'st rest;
Leaf-laden dryads, too, in verdure drest.
A strange weird world such forest was to thee,
Where mingled truth and dreams in mystery;
There leaned old ruminating pines, and there
The giant elms, whose boughs deformed and bare
A hundred rough and crooked elbows made;
And in this somber group the wind had swayed,
Nor life, nor death, but life in death seemed
    found.
The cresses drink, the water flows, and round
Upon the slopes the mountain rowans meet,
And 'neath the brushwood plant their gnarled
    feet,
Intwining slowly where the creepers twine.
There, too, the lakes as mirrors brightly shine,
And show the swan-necked flowers, each line by
    line.
Chimeras roused take stranger shapes for thee·
The glittering scales of mailèd throat we see,
And claws tight pressed on huge old knotted tree,
While from a cavern dim the bright eyes glare.
O vegetation! Spirit! Do we dare
Question of matter, and of forces found
'Neath a rude skin, in living verdure bound?
O master! I, like thee, have wandered oft
Where mighty trees made arches high aloft,
But ever with a consciousness of strife,
A surging struggle of the inner life;
Ever the trembling of the grass, I say,
And the boughs rocking as the breezes play,
Have stirred deep thoughts in a bewild'ring way.

O God! alone great witness of all deeds,
Of thoughts and acts, and all our human needs—
God only knows how often in such scenes
Of savage beauty under leafy screens
I've felt the mighty oaks had spirit dower,
Like me knew mirth and sorrow, sentient power,
And, whisp'ring each to each in twilight dim,
Had hearts that beat, and owned a soul from
　　Him!

————

TO HIS MUSE

SINCE everything below
　　Doth, in this mortal state,
Its tone, its fragrance, or its glow
　　Communicate;

Since all that lives and moves
　　Upon the earth, bestows
On what it seeks and what it loves
　　Its thorn or rose;

Since April to the trees
　　Gives a bewitching sound,
And somber night to grief gives ease,
　　And peace profound·

Since day-spring on the flower
　　A fresh'ning drop confers,
And the fresh air on branch and
　　　bower
　　Its choristers;

Since the dark wave bestows
    A soft caress, imprest
On the green bank to which it goes
    Seeking its rest—

I give thee at this hour,
    Thus fondly bent o'er thee,
The best of all the things in dow'r
    That in me be.

Receive—poor gift, 'tis true,
    Which grief, not joy, endears—
My thoughts, that like a shower of
        dew
    Reach thee in tears.

My vows untold receive,
    All pure before thee laid;
Receive of all the days I live
    The light or shade;

My hours with rapture filled,
    Which no suspicion wrongs;
And all the blandishments distilled
    From all my songs;

My spirit, whose essay
    Flies fearless, wild, and free,
And hath, and seeks, to guide its way
    No star but thee.

No pensive, dreamy Muse,
    Who, though all else should smile;
Oft   as   thou   weep'st,   with   thee
        would choose
    To weep the while.

O sweetest mine! this gift
Receive—'tis thine alone—
My heart, of which there's nothing
    left
When Love is gone!

————

THE COW

BEFORE the farm where o'er the porch festoon
Wild creepers red, and gaffer sits at noon,
While strutting fowl display their varied crests,
And the old watchdog slumberously rests,
They, half-attentive to the clarion of their king,
Resplendent in the sunshine op'ning wing—
There stood a cow, with neck-bell jingling light,
Superb, enormous, dappled red and white;
Soft, gentle, patient as a hind unto its young,
Letting the children swarm until they hung
Around her, under—rustics, with their teeth
Whiter than marble their ripe lips beneath,
And bushy hair fresh and more brown
Than mossy walls at old gates of a town,
Calling to one another with loud cries
For younger imps to be in at the prize;
Stealing without concern, but tremulous with fear
They glance around lest Doll the maid appear;
Their jolly lips, that haply cause some pain,
And all those busy fingers, pressing now and
    'gain
The teeming udders, whose small, thousand pores
Gush out the nectar 'mid their laughing roars,

While she, good mother, gives and gives in
    heaps,
And never moves. Anon there creeps
A vague soft shiver o'er the hide unmarred,
As sharp they pull; she seems of stone most hard.
Dreamy, of large eye, seeks she no release,
And shrinks not while there's one still to appease.

Thus Nature—refuge 'gainst the slings of fate!
Mother of all, indulgent as she's great!—
Lets us, the hungered of each age and rank,
Shadow and milk seek in the eternal flank;
Mystic and carnal, foolish, wise, repair—
The souls retiring and those that dare,
Sages with halos, poets laurel-crowned,
All creep beneath or cluster close around,
And with unending greed and joyous cries,
From sources full draw need's supplies,
Quench hearty thirst, obtain what must eftsoon
Form blood and mind, in freest boon,
Respire at length thy sacred, flaming light,
From all that greets our ears, touch, scent, or
    sight—
Brown leaves, blue mountains, yellow gleams,
    green sod—
Thou undistracted still dost dream of God.

THE PAST

THE pile was of the thirteenth Louis' days;
    Red sunset glowed the dismal palace round;

Each far-off window seemed a fiery blaze—
Unseen its shape, hid in a crimson haze—
And in the gleam the lofty roof was drowned.

Stretched 'neath our eyes, its ancient glory
flown,
A park where grass o'er every pathway
swarms;
And in some niche with ivy half o'ergrown,
Winter, grim statue! on a gray, worn stone,
Her hands above a marble fire warms.

In slumber lay the solitary lake,
Where moulded a gaunt Neptune, green with
slime;
Reeds hid the water which the banks did break,
And trees their ancient solemn branches shake,
Where erst did Boileau muse his learned
rhyme.

At times you saw stags in the forest range,
Who seemed to linger for the hunter's cry;
And propped by stumps, white marbles, lost and
strange,
Mixed with the hedgerow trees — ignoble
change!—
Twin sisters (Gabriel, Venus) mourn and
sigh.

Cloaks from whose lifted folds long rapiers peep
No longer in that voiceless garden stood·
The Tritons seem to shut their eyes and sleep;
A cavern its strong jaws doth open keep,
And yawns a-weary in the lonely wood.

And then I said, This palace lone and sad
　Held love as bright as in your heart can shine;
Fame, glory, laughter, endless feasting, had;
And all those vanished joys now sorrow add,
　As vessels rust and blacken from their wine.

Within that hollow, where the mosses crawl,
　Came, with drooped eyes and palpitating heart,
The beauteous Caussade, or the young Candale,
Who of a royal lover, willing thrall,
　Said "Sire" on entering, "Louis" when they
　　part.

There, as to-day, for Candale or Caussade,
　White, fleecy clouds in the blue heaven
　　streamed;
Soft golden rays upon the roof were spread,
A blaze of light was from the windows shed,
　And the sun sweetly smiled, and Nature
　　dreamed.

Then, as to-day, two hearts that one became,
　Did through these glades, to love devoted, stray.
His duchess all angelic he would name;
Eyes darting sparkling rays, and eyes of flame,
　Each fuel found in each, then as to-day.

In the far wood vague sounds of laughter rise—
　'Twas other lovers steeped in happiness.
Sometimes would silence hush their ecstasies,
And tenderly he asks, "Whence come your
　　sighs?"
　She softly answers, "Whence your thought-
　　fulness?"

The charmer and the king, hands interlaced,
   Trod the green sward in proud and glad de-
      light;
Their looks, their breath, their thoughts and
      hearts embraced.
O vanished times!   O splendors all effaced!
   O suns now sunk away in dismal night!

MOTHERS

SEE all the children gathered there,
Their mother near; so young, so fair,
   An elder sister she might be,
And yet she hears, amid their games,
The shaking of their unknown names
   In the dark urn of destiny.

She wakes their smiles, she soothes their
      cares,
On that pure heart so like to theirs;
   Her spirit with such life is rife
That in its golden rays we see,
Touched into graceful poesy,
   The dull, cold commonplace of life.

Still following, watching, whether burn
The Christmas log in winter stern,
   While merry plays go round,
Or streamlets laugh to breeze of May
That shakes the leaf to break away—
   A shadow falling to the ground.

If some poor man with hungry eyes
Her baby's coral bauble spies,
  She marks his look with famine wild;
For Christ's dear sake she makes with joy
An alms-gift of the silver toy,
  A smiling angel of the child.

LOVE'S TREACHEROUS POOL

DEAR child, at first dear love's a mirror bright
Whereo'er fair women bend with fond delight
  For bold or timorous gazing;
With heavenly beams each heart it doth fulfill,
Making all good things lovelier, all things ill
  From the rapt soul erasing.

Then one bends nearer, 'tis a pool, and then
A deep abysm! and clinging hands are vain,
  To banks frail flowers are crowning.
Charming is love, but deadly! Fear it, sweet:
In a river first the foolish little feet
  Dip; then a fair form's drowning!

TO SOME BIRDS FLOWN AWAY

CHILDREN, come back! come back, I say,
You whom my folly chased away
A moment since, from this my room,
With bristling wrath and words of doom!
What had you done, you bandits small,
With lips as red as roses all?

What crime?   What wild and hapless deed?
What porcelain vase by you was split
To thousand pieces?   Did you need
    For pastime, as you handled it,
Some Gothic missal to enrich
    With your designs fantastical?
Or did your tearing fingers fall
On some old picture?   Which, oh, which
Your dreadful fault?   Not one of these:
Only when left yourselves to please
This morning but a moment here
    'Mid papers tinted by my mind,
You took some embryo verses near—
    Half formed, but fully well designed
To open out.   Your heart's desire
Was but to throw them on the fire,
Then watch the tinder, for the sight
Of shining sparks that twinkle bright
As little boats that sail at night,
Or like the window lights that spring
From out the dark at evening.

'Twas all, and you were well content.
Fine loss was this for anger's vent!
A strophe ill made midst your play,
Sweet sound that chased the words away
In stormy flight.   An ode quite new
With rhymes inflated, stanzas too,
That panted, moving lazily,
    And heavy Alexandrine lines
That seemed to jostle bodily,
    Like children full of play designs
That spring at once from schoolroom's form.

Instead of all this angry storm,
Another might have thanked you well
For saving prey from that grim cell,
That hollowed den, 'neath journals great,
 Where editors who poets flout
 With their demoniac laughter shout.
And I have scolded you! What fate
For charming dwarfs, who never meant
 To anger Hercules! And I
Have frightened you! My chair I sent
 Back to the wall, and then let fly
A shower of words the envious use.
"Get out!" I said, what hard abuse ·
"Leave me alone—alone I say!"
Poor man, alone! Ah, well-a-day,
What fine result, with triumph rare!
 As one turns from the coffin'd dead
So left you me: I could but stare
 Upon the door through which you fled—
I proud and grave, but punished quite.
And what care you for this my plight?
You have recovered liberty,
Fresh air, and lovely scenery;
The spacious park and wished-for grass;
 The running stream, where you can throw
A blade to watch what comes to pass;
 Blue sky, and all the spring can show;
Nature, serenely fair to see;
The book of birds and spirits free—
God's poem, worth much more than mine,
Where flowers for perfect stanzas shine;
Flowers that a child may pluck in play,
No harsh voice frightening it away.

And I'm alone, all pleasure o'er—
   Alone with pedant called "Ennui";
For since the morning at my door
   Ennui has waited patiently.
That doctor, London born you mark,
One Sunday in December dark—
Poor little ones, he loved you not,
And waited till the chance he got
To enter as you passed away;
   And in the very corner where
You played with frolic-laughter gay,
   He sighs and yawns with weary air.

What can I do? Shall I read books,
Or write more verse, or turn fond looks
Upon enamels blue, sea-green,
And white; on insects rare, as seen
Upon my Dresden china ware?
Or shall I touch the globe, and care
To make the heavens turn upon
Its axis? No, not one—not one
Of all these things care I to do;
All wearies me: I think of you.
In truth, with you my sunshine fled,
And gayety with your light tread—
Glad noise that set me dreaming still.
'Twas my delight to watch your will,
And mark you point with finger-tips
   To help your spelling out a word;
To see the pearls between your lips
   When I your joyous laughter heard;
Your honest brows that looked so true,
   And said, "Oh, yes!" to each intent;

Your great bright eyes, that loved to view
  With admiration innocent
My fine old Sèvres; the eager thought
That every kind of knowledge sought;
The elbow push with "Come and see!"

Oh, certes! spirits,sylphs, there be,
And fays the wind blows often here.
The gnomes that squat the ceiling near,
In corners made by old books dim;
The long-backed dwarfs, those goblins grim
That seem at home 'mong vases rare,
And chat to them with friendly air—
Oh, how the joyous demon throng
Must all have laughed with laughter long
To see you on my rough draughts fall?
My bald hexameters, and all
The mournful, miserable band,
And drag them with relentless hand
From òut their box, with true delight
To set them each and all a-light,
And then with clapping hands to lean
Above the stove and watch the scene,
How to the mass deformed there came
A soul that showed itself in flame!

Bright tricksy children, oh, I pray,
Come back and sing and dance away,
And chatter too; sometimes you may,
A giddy group, a big book seize;
Or sometimes, if it so you please,
With nimble step you'll run to me
  And push the arm that holds the pen,

Till on my finished verse will be
  A stroke that's like a steeple when
Seen suddenly upon a plain.
My soul longs for your breath again
To warm it.   Oh, return! come here
With laugh and babble, and no fear
  When with your shadow you obscure
  The book I read; for I am sure,
Oh, madcaps terrible and dear,
That you were right and I was wrong.
But who has ne'er with scolding tongue
Blamed out of season.   Pardon me!
You must forgive, for sad are we.
The young should not be hard and cold
And unforgiving to the old.
Children, each morn your souls ope out
  Like windows to the shining day.
Oh, miracle that comes about—
  The miracle that children gay
Have happiness and goodness too.
Caressed by destiny are you'
  Charming you are, if you but play.
But we with living overwrought,
And full of grave and somber thought,
Are snappish oft; dear little men,
We have ill-tempered days, and then
Are quite unjust and full of care.
It rained this morning, and the air
Was chill; but clouds that dimmed the sky
Have passed.   Things spited me, and why?
But now my heart repents.   Behold
What 'twas that made me cross, and scold!
All by-and-by you'll understand,

When brows are marked by Time's stern
    hand;
Then you will comprehend, be sure,
When older—that's to say, less pure

The fault I freely own was mine,
But, oh, for pardon now I pine!
Enough my punishment to meet.
You must forgive; I do entreat
With clasped hands praying—oh,come back!
Make peace, and you shall nothing lack.
See now my pencils, paper, here,
And pointless compasses, and dear
Old lacquer-work, and stoneware clear
Through glass protecting—all man's toys
So coveted by girls and boys;
Great china monsters, bodies much
Like cucumbers, you all shall touch.
I yield up all! my picture rare
    Found beneath antique rubbish heap;
My great and tapestried oak chair
    I will from you no longer keep;
You shall about my table climb,
    And dance, or drag, without a cry
From me as if it were a crime;
    Even I'll look on patiently
If you your jagged toys all throw
Upon my carved bench till it show
The wood is torn; and freely, too,
I'll leave in your own hands to view
My pictured Bible—oft desired,
But which to touch your fear inspired—
With God in emperor's robes attired.

Then if to see my verses burn
Should seem to you a pleasant turn,
Take them to freely tear away
Or burn.   But, oh, not so I'd say,
If this were Méry's room to-day,
That noble poet!   Happy town,
Marseilles the Greek, that him doth own!
Daughter of Homer, fair to see,
Of Virgil's son the mother she.
To you I'd say, Hold, children all!
Let but your eyes on his work fall.
These papers are the sacred nest
In which his crooning fancies rest;
To-morrow winged to heaven they'll soar.
　For new-born verse imprisoned still
In manuscript may suffer sore
　At your small hands and childish will.
Without a thought of bad intent,
Of cruelty quite innocent,
You wound their feet and bruise their wings,
And make them suffer those ill things
That children's play to young birds brings.

But mine! no matter what you do,
My poetry is all in you;
You are my inspiration bright
That gives my verse its purest light.
Children, whose life is made of hope,
Whose joy, within its mystic scope,
Owes all to ignorance of ill,
You have not suffered, and you still
Know not what gloomy thoughts weigh down
The poet-writer weary grown.

What warmth is shed by your sweet smile!
How much he needs to gaze a while
Upon your shining placid brow,
When his own brow its ache doth know;
With what delight he loves to hear
Your frolic play 'neath tree that's near,
Your joyous voices mixing well
With his own song's all-mournful swell!
Come back, then, children! come to me,
If you wish not that I should be
As lonely now that you're afar
As fisherman of Etrétat,
Who listless on his elbow leans
Through all the weary winter scenes,
As tired of thought, as on time flies,
And watching only rainy skies!

MY THOUGHTS OF YE

What do I dream of? Far from the low roof,
Where now ye are, children, I dream of you;
Of your young heads that are the hope and crown
Of my full summer, ripening to its fall—
Branches whose shadow grows along my wall
Sweet souls scarce open to the breath of day,
Still dazzled with the brightness of your dawn.
I dream of those two little ones at play,
Making the threshold vocal with their cries,
Half tears, half laughter, mingled sport and strife,
Like two flowers knocked together by the wind:
Or of the elder two—more anxious thought—
Breasting already broader waves of life,

A conscious innocence on either face—
My pensive daughter and my curious boy.
Thus do I dream while the light sailors sing,
At even moored beneath some steepy shore,
While the waves opening all their nostrils breathe
A thousand sea-scents to the wandering wind,
And the whole air is full of wondrous sounds,
From sea to strand, from land to sea, given back.
Alone and sad, thus do I dream of you—
Children and house and home, the table set,
The glowing hearth, and all the pious care
Of tender mother, and of grandsire kind.
And while before me, spotted with white sails,
The limpid ocean mirrors all the stars,
And while the pilot, from the infinite main,
Looks with calm eye into the infinite heaven,
I, dreaming of you only, seek to scan
And fathom all my soul's deep love for you—
Love sweet and powerful and everlasting—
And find that the great sea is small beside it.

THE BEACON IN THE STORM

HARK, what somber tones!
From far billows dying,
Listen, hollow sighing,
Blent with heavy moans,
Blent with eerie crying,
Till a shriller wail
Bodes new agony:
Through his horn the gale
Thunders o'er the sea.

Rain in torrents, hark!
 On the low shore yonder
 Billows die in thunder
'Neath a heaven all dark,
 While with dread we wonder
Winter should prevail
 Ere his time to be:
Through his horn the gale
Thunders o'er the sea.

O lost mariners!
 While the ship doth founder,
 Through the darkness round her
Toward the shore one nears
 (Ay, the low shore yonder!)
Brawny arms—how frail!—
 Stretched out helplessly ·
Through his horn the gale
Thunders o'er the sea.

O rash mariners!
 While the ship's on-driven,
 Sail on sail shrieks, riven
As with tooth or shears.
 Not a star in heaven!
Strife's of none avail:
 Deadly rocks to lee!
Through his horn the gale
Thunders o'er the sea.

Lo! what sudden light?
 'Tis the star beholden,
 Brighter than all golden
Stars that gem the night—
 Torch God fires to embolden

Mariners who hail
It, while threateningly
Through his horn the gale
Thunders o'er the sea.

THE ROSE AND THE GRAVE

THE Grave said to the Rose:
"What of the dews of dawn,
  Love's flower, what end is theirs?"
"And what of spirits flown—
The souls whereon doth close
  The tomb's mouth unawares?"
The Rose said to the Grave.

The Rose said· "In the shade
From the dawn's tears is made
  A perfume faint and strange,
  Amber and honey sweet."
"And all the spirits fleet
Do suffer a sky change,
More strangely than the dew,
To God's own angels new,"
  The Grave said to the Rose.

END OF VOLUME SEVENTEEN

Printed in Great Britain
by Amazon